TOYOTA

This book is the third in the series *Japanese Business: The Human Face*, which will examine the most important companies in Japan today. These companies are all global leaders with multi-billion dollar turnovers and thousands of employees. Yet they face unprecedented challenges in the next few years. The pace of globalization, technical development, consumer expectation and growing international competition has never been faster. This series shows how the best and most successful are adapting and changing to remain in front. Each book describes the company's strategy, organization change and its impact on the workforce, and, most importantly, the importance of leadership in steering the company into the next millennium. These books contain crucial lessons for anyone interested in organizations, business and managing change.

Titles published in the series *Japanese Business: The Human Face*
Canon by Philip Sandoz
Mitsubishi Electric by Sol Sanders
Toyota: People, Ideas and the Challenge of the New by Edwin M. Reingold

JAPANESE BUSINESS
THE HUMAN FACE

TOYOTA

People, Ideas and the
Challenge of the New

EDWIN M. REINGOLD

PENGUIN BOOKS

Published by the Penguin Group
Penguin Books Ltd, 27 Wrights Lane, London w8 5tz, England
Penguin Putnam Inc., 375 Hudson Street, New York, New York 10014, USA
Penguin Books Australia Ltd, Ringwood, Victoria, Australia
Penguin Books Canada Ltd, 10 Alcorn Avenue, Toronto, Ontario, Canada m4v 3b2
Penguin Books (NZ) Ltd, Private Bag 102902, NSMC, Auckland, New Zealand

Penguin Books Ltd, Registered Offices: Harmondsworth, Middlesex, England

First published 1999
1 3 5 7 9 10 8 6 4 2

Copyright © IRI Inc., 1999

Set in 11.5/14pt Monotype Bembo
Typeset by Rowland Phototypesetting Ltd, Bury St Edmunds, Suffolk
Printed and bound in Great Britain by Clays Ltd, St Ives plc

A CIP catalogue record for this book is available from the British Library

ISBN 0-140-28591-1

Contents

Preface

When I reported on the American motor industry for *Time* magazine in the oil-crisis years of the 1970s, Japanese automobiles were beginning to make serious inroads in the market, and Detroit executives were only moderately concerned. They reasoned that about 15 per cent of the American new car market was captured each year by foreign makers – British, German, Swedish, French and Japanese. The general industry view was that the foreign makers were primarily in the small-car end of the market, which US makers did not find profitable. And in the oft-repeated words of a former chairman of Chrysler Corporation, Lynn Townsend, 'The American people do not want a small car.'

Japanese imports had an uneven history in the US. The early versions sent overseas were of poor quality and worse performance. They had been laughed off America's high-speed freeways. One shipment of early Datsun (now called Nissan) cars were severely damaged on the way to the American port by a rather vicious Pacific Ocean storm, and surprisingly the Datsun salesmen were relieved. 'We realized we could get the insurance and wouldn't have to try to sell them,' recalls one. Grudgingly, however, US makers were admitting that the quality had improved with experience. But, as a General Motors vice-president told me with a sneer, most buyers of imported cars want the cachet of owning a foreign car and would buy one no matter what models Detroit offered. This was an attitude that was soon to change. Foreign car sales – and especially Japanese car sales – began to soar in the wake of the oil embargo imposed by the Organization of Petroleum Exporting Countries (OPEC) after the 1973 Arab–Israeli war. When Japanese sales threatened to reach 25 per cent of the US market, Detroit was finally aroused. As they pleaded with the US Congress for protection from the onslaught of Japanese imports, they began to show interest in the Japanese 'secret'.

The secret? What, many of them asked, was the trick, the gimmick, the special thing that enabled the Japanese makers to produce well-made and attractive cars and sell them at bargain prices overseas? Was it automation, computers, robots, lifetime employment, seniority-based wages, quality circles, suggestion systems, government export subsidies and other incentives, or some ineffable cultural trait of the Japanese? And what of Japanese labour and its no-strike loyalty to employers, wasn't that part of it? The answer, of course, was that there is no secret at all. It was some, but not all, of the above and more, but the key factor was people with ideas, determination and dedication, and hard-working colleagues open to those ideas and happy to share their own. It was a labour force accustomed to hard work and sacrifice. It was not exactly rocket science, after all, but innovative thinking and people willing to invest an idea with their sweat and brainpower. Not every Japanese manufacturer was equally successful, and some that were successful for a time have faltered, yet today eleven companies build cars in Japan. A single man's vision can plant the seed of a great corporation but it takes many people of determination and dedication to nurture it, make it grow, and keep it ahead of the competition. A necessary factor was aid from banks and government – low-interest loans and market protection and export subsidies enabled an industry to develop.

A now-famous five-year study of the world automobile industry by researchers at the Massachusetts Institute of Technology's International Motor Vehicle Program concluded finally in 1990 that the so-called 'secret weapon' of the Japanese was a unique manufacturing system that could be, and indeed would be, employed worldwide. It was a system made in Japan, by Japanese, but applicable everywhere. As for the leading, but unnamed, company in the survey, its system originated from ideas gleaned not from some special Japanese wellspring of philosophy but from earlier visits to American auto factories and US super-markets.

The researchers, James P. Womack, Daniel T. Jones and Daniel Roos, said in their non-partisan 1990 report, *The Machine That Changed the World*, was that the pioneer and leader in the development and implementation of what has become known as 'Lean Manufacturing' was Japan's Toyota Motor Corporation. In their 1996 book titled *Lean Thinking*, Womack and Jones wrote that by 1990 Toyota had become the pre-eminent production organ-ization in the world. But they also pointed out that this was no overnight gimmick, that it took Toyota thirty-five years to put in place the interconnected system known as the Toyota Production System and that it is still not without flaw, a fact Toyota people readily volunteer.

Today Toyota employs its technologies at home and abroad, is teaching the system to any company that seeks to know of it, including competitors, and has set up an organization in the United States for this purpose. Now the corporation is expanding the system in its European operations. It is no longer a Japanese secret but an international open book. The system is more than a way to put pieces together; it is a means of orienting all aspects of the venture toward a concerted goal. Founded in 1937 as a remote dream, Toyota grew to become the third largest auto maker in the world, on the heels of General Motors and Ford of the US, this position being challenged only by the 1998 merger of the Chrysler Corporation and Germany's Daimler Benz. From humble beginnings in a rural town in central Japan, Toyota has risen to become a globe-girdling network of 40 overseas car-making facilities in 24 countries, selling motor vehicles in 160 countries and still growing as the nerve centre of 263 subsidiaries companies and 60 affiliated companies. Despite its size, Toyota is considered by some analysts to be the best-managed corporation in the world, albeit a company facing critical challenges. Sceptics say it cannot possibly keep its position as holder of so many superlatives while Japan itself changes demographically and as Toyota's founding leadership ages and younger hands take the wheel.

For the first time in three decades a president who is not a member of the founding family makes the corporation's crucial decisions with the help of his talented and experienced advisers and he is setting the company on a new course. In its home market, with several competitors (there are eleven car makers on the domestic scene), Toyota has been struggling to maintain its historic 40 per cent of the market, while expanding its manufacturing network into continental Europe to conquer a bigger chunk of that new single currency market.

Bold outlines have been sketched for the twenty-first century, and the first steps have been taken on the road to full global status: a new factory in Europe and, a new dual-mode hybrid car, the first of its kind to be offered in the mass market. Research and development on novel electric vehicles to be powered by fuel cells is ongoing. A unique transportation system for vehicles and special roadways is being developed. Experiments continue on automotive and non-automotive ways to improve the environment. Marine and aviation ventures are being pursued, as well as new production methods for handsome prefabricated home-building. New approaches to manufacturing, marketing and selling are also being stimulated to prepare for the challenges of the increasingly interconnected world of the years ahead.

Change, then, is in the air. But even as the executives talk of new ventures, new alliances and the latest in science and technology, above all Toyota is a $100 billion corporation that makes cars.

What follows is a glimpse of the people around the world who created and now nurture the industrial organization seen as the benchmark of the world's auto industry: in short, the human face of the Toyota Motor Corporation.

★ ★ ★

As this book was going to press, Toyota Motor Corporation announced its intention to make key changes at the management level around the third quarter of 1999. President Hiroshi Okuda, whose decisive moves toward modernization and internationaliz-ation are discussed in the pages that follow, is scheduled to become chairman of the corporation and executive vice-president Fujio Cho president. In announcing the planned changes, chairman Shoichiro Toyoda said that in the new structure the chairman will act as chief executive officer of the corporation and the new president as chief operating officer. It is an executive arrangement common in US and European companies but rare in Japan.

Under the plan, Toyoda would become honorary chairman, the post now held by his cousin, Eiji Toyoda, who would be named chief advisor. Okuda is credited with achieving a return to Toyota's dominant position in the domestic auto market, capturing just over 40 per cent, and with setting the corporation on a broader international course. Cho, who figures prominently in the pages that follow has said he will pursue the same goals.

Introduction

The world's love–hate relationship with the automobile has taken many forms since Captain Nicolas Cugnot frightened the horses of Paris with the first self-propelled motor vehicle more than two hundred years ago. His cantankerous, hissing steam-powered three-wheeler was a curious behemoth of a machine that could hardly have given those who saw it in action in 1769 any notion of what was to come. It would be many long years before man's ingenuity could produce a reasonable prototype of the modern automobile.

Praised and damned today in a hundred languages, the auto is derided as an instrument of death, blamed for everything from the fouling of the earth's atmosphere and the pollution of its surface, to teen pregnancy. Yet today autos continue to be accepted as symbols of success for the middle class, toys of the rich and powerful and those who aspire to be. In the world's biggest single market, the affluent United States, some well-off parents congratulate high-school graduates with their first car. Husbands and wives are known to wrap a giant ribbon around an automotive anniversary gift. In Hollywood, exuberant movie moguls even shower expensive luxury convertibles on colleagues to celebrate a successful venture.

The blandishments of the automobile companies – excitement, status, economy, comfort, safety, efficiency – flood the television channels. Advertisements in newspapers, magazines, on billboards and, of course, on the internet, are inescapable. Over the years, automobile sales rise and falter, but the curve continues inexorably upward, even in the face of increasingly stringent safety and emissions standards. When a market is considered saturated there is still the need to replace older, less safe and less efficient vehicles with something newer, safer, more efficient, and, let's face it, better looking.

Politically, cars have risen beyond their utilitarian origins to become symbols of national success as well. Governments of developing nations often look upon a locally assembled automobile as a ticket for admission into the club of advanced nations. The weight of an industry that produces high value-added products and provides employment is not inconsiderable in national capitals. Nations that have lost such an industry have found their citizens eager to allow, even to entice, foreign makers to revive it.

Since M. Cugnot departed the scene, the automobile has been 'invented' many times over in many lands. In Britain, Robert Davidson built a practical electric vehicle in 1873. Steam-powered cars were popular in Britain as public conveyances even after the first gasoline engine-powered cars were produced on the Continent. Parliament wasn't too keen on the idea of motoring. For sixty years, until 1896, the Red Flag Act required someone carrying a red flag (or red lantern at night) to precede any self-propelled vehicle. In the United States, the Stanley brothers produced a Steamer that set a world speed record of over 120 miles an hour, but in 1885 Karl Benz built the first automobile powered by a four-cycle internal combustion gasoline engine. That engine, invented by Nikolaus August Otto, was the forerunner of the main power source of almost all of today's autos. Benz's car was a three-wheeler steered by means of a tiller. Within a year, his countryman Gottlieb Daimler improved on Otto's engine and produced a four-wheel car. Five years later, a Frenchman named René Panhard produced a car with a configuration in which most automobiles operate today: the engine in front (instead of under the driver's seat) powering wheels at the rear through a drive-shaft. As ever-more exotic models were produced in Europe, it took the buggy-makers and tinkers of the United States to democratize and popularize the motor car. Opinion leaders were urging young men to 'go west', to travel afar in the sprawling and sparsely populated land. Americans fell in love with the possibility of personal mobility. But to go west, east, north or south, those young men, and women, needed personal transportation. They had their choice of steam-, electricity- and gasoline-powered vehicles, if they could afford them, for they were hand-made and expensive.

It was Henry Ford and his colleagues who gave them what they needed. Ford figured out how to make sturdy lookalike cars in mass quantities and sell them at a reasonable price to roamers and Sunday drivers alike. Ford's conveyor belt mass production system and the integration of manufacturing facilities became the envy of the automotive world.

In Japan, a nation that abandoned its self-imposed isolation of 250 years only in 1868, few citizens had seen an automobile until 1900, when the Japanese residents of San Francisco presented the crown prince a hand-made electric car as a wedding gift.

The end of the nineteenth century was a heady time in Japan. The nation was voraciously importing as much Western culture and technology as it could adapt to its own Japanese way of doing things, attempting to 'catch up' with the West. Some imports were gobbled up whole. The first railway line, built with foreign technology and rolling stock, was opened between Tokyo and Yokohama in 1872, and, although rail lines multiplied rapidly as citizens discovered the ease of travel, Japan, though even then heavily urbanized, remained largely a nation on foot.

Some of Japan's roads had been improved by local warlords for defensive military purposes during the period of isolation. Seventeenth-century strongman Nobunaga Oda built a network of twenty-foot-wide highways through his fiefdom of Owari in central Japan, around what is now Nagoya – and Toyota City. The roads were tree-lined, and crowned to drain in the rain, yet travellers described them as tortuous, often deep in spring's mud and dusty in the heat of summer. Shogun Ieyasu Tokugawa actually widened the Tokaido, the main route between the old capital of Kyoto and Tokyo (then known as Edo), to 33 feet and lined it with pine trees and cedars, but travel was still no joy ride.

Until the reform of 1868 the local lords, or *daimyo*, were kept virtually impoverished (and therefore militarily impotent) by the shogun's requirement that they leave their wives and families hostage in Edo and make biennial processions to the new capital to report to the palace. The trek was a matter of great pride, and therefore costly, done with panoply, a phalanx of warriors and retainers mainly on foot, flying the proud clan flags, horses carrying the considerable baggage load, and nobles riding in richly brocaded palanquins or litters. This grand travel, colourfully documented in woodblock prints by *ukiyoe* artists, was not without inconvenience. Four rivers cross the Tokaido but the wily shogun refused to build bridges over them. When the splendid entourages arrived at the water's edge, people and baggage had to be ferried across on the sturdy backs of professional porters. Only pilgrims and wrestlers were allowed to wade across the rivers. The system was great for commerce along the way, as it usually took two weeks to make the Kyoto to Edo trek, and the travellers had to be watered and fed. Wayside inns, perhaps the first Asian motels and fast food restaurants, prospered.

As late as 1872, a few years into the era named after the Emperor Meiji, Tokyo's main street, Ginza, had no sidewalks or formal carriageway. Within a few years all that would change. *Jinrikisha* (rickshaws) were the first vehicles involved in the modernization, followed by bicycles and carriages, and, later, horse-drawn trams. Shortly after the turn of the century one Komanosuke Uchiyama imported an 18-horsepower engine from the United States and used it to build a primitive bus. Soon bus routes served Osaka, and Kyoto and Hiroshima, as well as Tokyo. Well-to-do merchants began importing cars from Britain and the United States, and along with Western dress came the newly discovered delights of the taxicab.

In an instant, disaster struck a severe blow to the capital's infrastructure. The Great Kanto Earthquake levelled most of Tokyo on the first day of September 1923, wiping out the capital's transportation infrastructure. It paralysed the Tokyo bay area, and the damage extended to much of Yokohama. There was panic in the streets. At least 91,000 people were killed, 52,000 were injured and 13,000 were unaccounted for. Rail lines were upended. Most of the motor vehicles then in use were either crushed under falling buildings or destroyed in the devastating fires that followed the tremor. Except for hand–drawn vehicles there was almost no available transportation. The government seized upon a solution: a rush order went off to Detroit for 800 Model T Ford chassis.

Within a few years both Ford and General Motors were assembling vehicles in Japan for the local market, using imported parts. Ford opened its factory in 1925 and General Motors in 1927. Masters of adaptation and innovation, the Japanese eyed the outpouring of these assembly plants enviously, and a Japanese motor vehicle industry was not long in coming.

Tokyo's second destruction, by US fire-bombing in 1945, was in some ways a repeat of the devastation of the 1923 earthquake. Over 100,000 people were killed in the firestorms that literally boiled the canals of the capital and burned all but the sturdiest concrete structures, which were few. When it was over, the rebuilding began, with salvaged cars and trucks fuelled by charcoal burners. The auto industry that had started tentatively in the 1930s, only to be commandeered by the military and its need for trucks, not passenger cars, had a chance for a second start at putting itself, and much of the world, on wheels. Doing it was to be quite a feat.

CHAPTER ONE
WEAVING A COMPANY

Students arrived early and filled all the seats in the lecture aud-
itorium. Late arrivals had to settle for a seat outside the Polymer
Institute hall, to watch the proceedings on a closed-circuit television monitor. The local press showed up, as well as a gaggle
of local businessmen. 'We tried to discourage people from
coming when we saw how big it was going to get,' says Jim
Barnett, the event organizer. Still they kept coming.

This was Akron, Ohio, a city once known as the rubber capital
of the world, a town whose industry put the American automobile
industry on rubber tyres, and now a centre for the research and
manufacture of polymers. It was no wonder, then, that the
attraction was no rock star, actor or popular sitcom celebrity but
a tall and athletic, serious-visaged Japanese named Hiroshi Okuda.
He came to this forum of the University of Akron's Institute for
Global Business to explain why he is kicking over the traces at
his own company, Toyota Motor Corporation, and setting new
goals for social responsibility in the industry of the twenty-first
century.

Unlike the practice in American corporations, in Japanese
firms the desk of the president, not the chairman, is where
the buck starts and stops. If anybody can order Toyota Motor
Corporation to change it is Okuda. Since becoming president
in 1995 Okuda has been a keen advocate of streamlining his
corporation, cutting back yet further on bureaucracy (a process
that has been going on for ten years), and hurling fresh challenges.
He has exhorted his employees to be creative, 'to challenge
established ways of doing things and create new ways and entities
by breaking with the *status quo*'. He counsels them not to be too

'haughty' or too proud to learn from others and to 'transcend organizational demarcations to get results, to pursue goals that appear to be just beyond your capabilities and to find new, untried pathways'.

New pathways for the hulking Toyota, a company often thought of as conservative, stuffy, slow to act, whose employees are often considered as bland and interchangeable as the parts of a car? Toyota, a company that arose in the industrial hinterlands of Japan, and was created by self-proclaimed country bumpkins? Unsophisticated as they were, compared with the city slickers of the industry, these hicks were pre-eminent in the automobile industry. Although the company has taken on the patina of worldliness, there is a kind of perverse pride among its executives, who often joke about being called *kintaro ame*, a confection that shows the same face of the folk hero Kintaro no matter where you slice it. And so Okuda's call for even more change is a stunning challenge for members of a company that has been undergoing a lot of it. But the global environment for the industry, and for the Toyota Motor, has been changing. The 1998 crisis in Asia was a shock to all Japanese auto makers, but, despite a sudden two-thirds drop in its Asian business, Toyota was still able to turn its accustomed profit, because of its healthy operations in North America and Europe. All the more reason, says Okuda, for speeding the true globalization of the company with new, major investments in the United States and Europe, and the importation of new faces and new ideas.

In his Akron appearance, and the same week at Yale University, Okuda outlined his view of the developmental history of change, the historical watersheds, that have taken place in the motor industry. The first era of change, he said, began with Henry Ford, who established a *de facto* standard with his new approach to product design and his flow production system. Ford's innovative conveyor line assembly system and the vertical integration of his company caught a fledgling industry unprepared to compete with it in 1913, but it established the standard for automobile manufacturing, and made the automobile 'a defining product of the twentieth century'.

'So Mr Ford developed a seemingly invincible advantage. But, as we all know, his advantage was not invincible. It succumbed partly to his understandable but narrow dedication to a highly successful business model. But it also yielded to the new business model that Alfred Sloan assembled at General Motors,' which included the concept of modern systematic marketing, a diversified line of closed-body sedans, and the cultivation of repeat customers. It additionally heralded the introduction of annual styling changes to motivate customers to buy cars.

Also importantly, said Okuda, is that Sloan's business model rested on 'his sophisticated perspective on financial management. He declared outright that the purpose of business was to increase return on investment and he shaped his company systematically to fulfil that purpose.' In contrast, Ford declared that 'profit is the "inevitable conclusion of work well done" '. His view of the profit motive became the view of most Japanese: that profit came after product and good work. According to Okuda, Ford warned that 'money gets itself ahead of service' when profits are over-emphasized.

Yet Okuda paid homage to Ford and Sloan as men who single-handedly shaped their times. Both men, he said, made contributions that continue to shape modern industry and for many years their books were required reading at the Toyota Motor Corporation.

'Another watershed occurred when Japanese auto makers introduced two important concepts in manufacturing and marketing.' Now Okuda was getting to the point. 'In manufacturing they changed Henry Ford's concept of flow production with the principles of just-in-time management. And they used *kanban* and other tools to tie all the production processes directly to actual market demand. In marketing, the Japanese makers demonstrated the global economics of scale that became possible in the post-war system of free trade and stable exchange rates.' American makers early on found it impractical to export because of tariffs, high shipping costs and currency issues, among other impediments, so they localized. Henry Ford set up a factory in Britain as early as 1911. But after the Second World War, in contrast, noted Okuda, 'The Japanese auto makers, like other Japanese manufacturers, became exporters. We centralized R&D and manufacturing in Japan and served global markets from a single location. This is how it grew.'

They were able to do this largely because of stable currencies and, especially in the United States, open borders and low tariffs. Then came the 1980s, when trade frictions intensified in the face of the rising popularity of Japanese products in the US. American companies began to invest in Japanese companies, and American auto executives, such as Lee Iacocca of the Chrysler Corporation, taunted the Japanese industry with the slogan: 'If you want to sell them in America, come and make them in America.' Before Toyota took up the challenge and began to produce vehicles in the US, Iacocca wrote, 'I'm a great admirer of the Japanese. Why? Because they know where they've come from, they know where they're at, and they know where they're going. And, most important, they have a national strategy to get them there. They also know how to make good cars. During the 1970s their cars were actually better than ours. That's not true any longer, but many Americans still believe it.'

The reigning strategy of each era seemed invincible for a time, Okuda pointed out, but changing circumstances modified each era and each philosophy, and yielded to a new model. Those circumstances are changing once more. 'We will need to find new ways to grow and prosper in the coming century. We need to decentralize our manufacturing and R&D activities on account of political sensitivities and volatile exchange rates. The product and process paradigms that Henry Ford established are themselves breaking down. Growing concern for the environment will stimulate new innovation and occasion new product paradigms. Information technology is transforming the inner workings of the automobile and also is transforming the way we develop and make and sell our products, and the growing role of information technology will open up our industry to a vast range of new competitors.'

To illustrate the magnitude of the transformation, Okuda noted to his Akron audience that until the 1980s nearly all Toyota manufacturing and all key decision-making was done within a twenty-mile radius of Toyota City. 'Senior managers all had the same perspective, the same world view. They all worked in the same town, ate at the same restaurants, played golf at the same courses. Now most of the cars we sell outside Japan come from plants outside Japan.' One lesson of the decentralization and globalization that has followed – as Okuda noted, of Toyota cars sold abroad, more than half are built abroad – is that it is no longer acceptable in foreign markets to sell vehicles that are not designed specifically for those markets, something American makers in Europe, such as Ford and General Motors, learned many years before. But that essential decentralization brings with it challenges: 'The biggest is the task of maintaining efficiency in decision-making. Consensus building is difficult when management functions are scattered over the world.'

Speaking about his own company and by implication the entire industry, he warned that managements must be careful to avoid being blinded by previous success, and must know 'when to opt for bold leaps instead of incremental steps'. Some in his company have not yet detached their mindset from the model of the 1970s and 1980s.

A big part of my job, said Okuda, 'is to keep Toyota from becoming a prisoner of success. That is why I am preaching change to everyone in our company. I am trying to show people that failure to change is even riskier than change itself. I am encouraging people to use their imagination and see the larger challenges that we face. I am urging them to meet those challenges with big new ideas rather than small improvements in old ideas.'

Okuda's ideas have challenged everybody in the company. He has called for nothing less than a corporate revolution. Employees are constantly reminded that environmental protection and resource conservation must be their concern, that corporations must develop and nurture revolutionary technologies and then create products that place less burden on the environment and that use minimal resources and energy. He has told his executives that protecting the environment 'is the most important issue Toyota corporate management must address' and has given this new corporate philosophy the title 'Harmonious Growth'. Toyota is a company that believes in and lives with its slogans and exhortations of mission, goals and values. They are emblazoned on signboards, on brass plaques, in company literature, and are discussed and debated seriously.

In an interview in Tokyo recently, a relaxed and smiling Okuda recalled an old Chinese proverb, that 'Everything lasts only forty years,' human beings or organizations. 'But if I come to think of it, it may be that in those days in China the average lifetime was only forty years, so nowadays I have revised it to sixty years. Toyota has just celebrated its sixtieth anniversary, and that means we are facing a period of cyclical crisis. I have coined the phrase "Second Foundation Era" because the first foundation era is over.'

In the new era, successful business models must include new values and new kinds of thinking, and that time has come. Toyota's two grand goals for the twenty-first century are to bring the automobile into 'metabolic harmony' with the natural environment, and the company into 'metabolic harmony' with the global community. It is not clear to everybody at Toyota – and certainly not to the sceptics outside the company who are put off by the unusual – just how this is to be achieved. Staff have been assigned and budgets allocated for a wide range of activities, as we shall see, not the least of which is the development of environmentally benign automobiles and transportation systems. Toyota design, research, manufacturing, distribution and sales assignments are performed by a global network of facilities manned by locals and Japanese.

Although Okuda is the first president in almost thirty years who is not related to the founding family – that family's name is Toyoda, but the company name was changed to Toyota for reasons we'll note later – he has the full confidence of the elder Toyoda executives of Toyota. He is not a timid man.

Looking back on his hiring by Toyota on his graduation from Tokyo's prestigious Hitotsubashi University, Okuda calls his selection 'just a coincidence. I just happened to join this business.' As is typical in Japan, company recruiters snap up potentially effective young graduates and exploit their natural abilities. They test them in a variety of jobs, sometimes out of their depth. Often it's sink or swim. Okuda was a swimmer. He grew up amid talk of stocks and bonds – his father ran a small brokerage firm – and, almost naturally, he majored in economics at university.

And so, at twenty-three, he was assigned, not surprisingly, to the Toyota accounting department, where he excelled, and then moved on to marketing. A theme repeated in Toyota's human-resource management is the constant shifting of executive personnel into untried areas of responsibility. The staffers become accustomed to making abrupt moves and facing new and often monumental challenges. And it helps to keep the corporate head count down. But opportunities reside in these assignments, as experience builds on experience. In 1973 Okuda was plucked out of his office job and sent to Manila to oversee one of Toyota's first offshore engine-manufacturing plants. It was a heady time in the Philippines under Ferdinand Marcos and his glamorous First Lady, Imelda, and Okuda remembers the era with eloquent simplicity. 'They were lavishly borrowing, spending, wasting money,' Okuda recalls. Toyota's Philippine partner in the engine plant – a local partner was always required for foreign ventures, as part of the Marcos system – was running a conglomerate, including ventures in mining, banking, insurance and a department store. 'We were kind of supporting, assisting the operations of this partner' – he pauses to chuckle – 'including a casino! I was young then, about forty, and if I had remained in Japan instead of going abroad I would never have had the opportunity to learn so many things first hand. I got to know high-ranking government officials. I was able to visit the Malacañan palace and learned to negotiate with government ministers. The experience was useful for me later when I went to the United States. I didn't hesitate to see high-ranking people.' The Philippines experience with the joint venture was also a training in worldly wisdom. Before Okuda left Tokyo a colleague told him to learn and study the Philippine people because all the problems of American society are reflected in miniature there.

Okuda came back to Japan, becoming general manager of the Asia and Oceania division in 1979 and was named a director of the company in 1982. Soon he was supervising a full range of international operations, including preparations for the construction of major plants in Taiwan and the United States. 'I had to go through a lot of negotiations in the US, meeting with state governors and federal government representatives. The experience in the Philippines turned out to be very useful,' he says, with a knowing smile. Okuda moved to the top in relatively short order, by Japanese corporate standards: from senior managing director in 1988 to executive vice-president in 1992 and three years later to president. As chief executive officer he not only shapes corporate policy for Toyota but also serves as a spokesman for the Japan auto industry and for Japanese manufacturing in general. He has earned a black belt in judo, though he no longer hits the mats, and has little time for golf; he makes as many as fifteen overseas trips a year and, of course, the job is never out of his mind. His work keeps him occupied '80 or 90 per cent of the time, and the other 10 per cent is listening to my wife complain' that she doesn't see him enough.

There are always decisions to be made, and 'I have to consider the possibility that if I do anything wrong in my management it would adversely influence the lives of many employees throughout the world. I feel a keen sense of responsibility.' Okuda has a large staff of executives to help him make decisions, but he says, 'I consult with many people but I think when it comes to decision-making I would have to make my own. One has to be responsible and accountable.

'For example, take vehicle design. I am a lay person when it comes to this, but we can't go ahead with a new design unless the president says yes. It's hard for even the designers to know which one will be a great success, even though they all believe in their own designs. So someone has to make the decision and that must be me. So, in the case of vehicle design, if it is successful the designer will get the credit; if it is not successful the president will have to take responsibility.' To be able to do that, he says, most of his day is spent 'immersed in business'. He has regular meetings once or twice a week with the elders of the company, former president (now chairman) Shoichiro Toyoda and his elder cousin, honorary chairman Eiji Toyoda. Both men are still active as company representatives but are out of the day-to-day decision-making process. 'When it comes to business operation, this is not something I would routinely discuss with the chairman or the honorary chairman; that would be determined by meeting with the vice-presidents.' He meets with them daily, either in the ageing, low-slung post-war home office building in Toyota City, an hour's drive from Nagoya, or in Toyota's soaring office building in Tokyo. The home office is an oasis of calm, in contrast to the nearby assembly plants with their bustling fork-lifts and bicycles, the showering sparks of welders, the clang and crunch of giant presses. In soft tones of greeting, the ubiquitous uniformed office ladies greet visitors with smiles and gloved-hand gestures. They glide effortlessly to escort a visitor to a conference or meeting-room. In the executive wing, the offices are open, and often empty, for there are, despite streamlining, endless meetings. Strict timetables are set, and adhered to, and so is the old-fashioned system of presenting refreshments – coffee, green tea, black tea, fruit juice, quietly delivered and placed before each participant unbidden. The servers withdraw silently, bowing to unheeding guests as they leave. The only sound is the hissing and click of the closing door.

Decision-making is never easy, with heavy responsibilities overshadowing each problem, but the key to making wise decisions, Okuda says, is in being informed.

In another context Toyota's dynamic new leader told his Ohio audience, 'Everything is obvious in hindsight. The trick is to keep your eyes open and learn to see.'

He was, with a touch of irony and nostalgia, paraphrasing something said a century previously by Sakichi Toyoda, the man whose ingenuity and dogged pursuit of his goals made the Toyota Motor Corporation possible: 'Open the window. It's a big world out there.'

BEGINNING

In the late nineteenth century Sakichi Toyoda, a young man living in a remote farming community may have seemed like an unlikely bet to create a giant industrial empire. But he had an inventive genius. The nation's new government plan to develop home-grown manufacturing created a system of cottage industries that to some extent exist partially even today in the shadow of the giants. Small machine shops and mills, with just a few employees, abound. The weaving of cotton cloth was thus spread into virtually every village; it was a way for housewives to earn some extra money during those lean years.

As Sakichi reminisced, 'The work was done by old women sitting at home and weaving the cloth by hand. Although everybody in my village was a farmer, every house had its own handloom.' With only an elementary education, Sakichi set about learning the carpentry trade of his father and turned his woodworking skills to improving the kind of looms that his mother laboured on. He grew so involved with redesigning looms that he neglected his carpentry, angering his father. 'People around me probably thought I was some kind of madman,' he recalled. Intent on improving on the old wooden looms, and aware of the new patent laws that could protect his designs, he travelled to Tokyo in 1890 to see the national industrial exhibition. It was eye-opening for the young man, who fancied himself an inventor. A year later he patented his first practical wooden loom, and claimed it increased productivity by 40–50 per cent. With his new looms Sakichi moved to Tokyo and started a weaving business. The cloth he wove became popular but the looms he wished to sell were not. The answer was to design a better loom. He designed many and by 1893 he was married and had a son named Kiichiro, who would eventually see his father's industrial vision come true.

Sakichi left his wife in Tokyo and moved back to his home village with his son to concentrate on newer inventions. He started a new company selling machines to reel cotton, but still devoted his attention to the development of an automatic power loom. Sakichi remarried in 1897, and his new wife, Asako Hayashi, raised Kiichiro and managed the family business, while Sakichi's younger brother Heikichi joined the firm as sales manager. The company prospered selling machines, and Sakichi was emboldened to open a weaving business with sixty new steam-powered looms, designed by himself.

Getting things mechanized in Japan led to some ingenious

solutions. Steam engines powered the mills of the day, but some spinning was done aboard large river boats that plied the river waters of Aichi's rivers. The power for the machines was supplied by giant paddle wheels on each side. Success at last began to crown Sakichi's efforts as the Mitsui trading company recognized the quality of his machines and signed a sales agreement. His new wooden looms cost a mere tenth of the similar German loom and a quarter of the next best French loom of its kind. More important, his power loom of 1896 had a cut-off device that shut it down when a malfunction such as a broken thread occurred.

But when Japan went to war against China in 1894, the country was hit by recession and the textile industry went into a nose-dive. Sakichi went back to his old company and continued to devise newer machines. Fortunes changed completely, however, when the Russo-Japanese war broke out in 1904. Demand for cotton cloth rose dramatically. Suddenly Toyoda's inexpensive power looms were again in demand. But his mind was concentrated on the idea of an automatic loom. His existing models were pitted against the best that British makers could produce in a test run by the company now known as Kanebo. Sakichi's looms came off second best. He was disappointed and angry, lamenting that he had allowed others to help build and test his looms.

'It is impossible to create an innovative product,' he wrote later, 'unless you do it yourself, pay attention to every detail, and then test it exhaustively. Never entrust the creation process of a product to others, for doing so will inevitably lead to failure and cause you deep regret.'

Regret, perhaps, and discouragement, but not defeat. In 1907 Sakichi established his own Toyoda Loom Works, with paid-in capital of one million yen. He resigned three years later and travelled to the United States, where he first saw the ubiquity of the automobile and was intrigued by the complexity of the machine. He liked to tinker and often noted to his son, Kiichiro,

'How can you do your job without getting your hands dirty?' (Kiichiro, who eventually succeeded in fulfilling his father's desire to build a Japanese automobile 'with Japanese hands', in turn wrote, just after the Second World War, 'I would have grave reservations about our ability to rebuild Japan's industry if our engineers were the type who could sit down to take their meals without ever having to wash their hands.')

Back home, Sakichi went into business in earnest, and with the First World War the need for his products again climbed. Soon Toyoda Spinning and Weaving Co., Ltd, was running 34,000 spindles, 1,000 looms and a staff of 1,000.

This, then, was the foundation of the Toyoda group of companies. It was to grow geometrically, and the low-cost Toyoda automatic looms and a line of other associated machinery were top-rated. In 1929 Kiichiro went to England to negotiate for the company with Platt Brothers, one of Britain's premier makers of spinning and weaving machinery. The British company purchased the world patent rights (with the exception of Japan, China and the United States) to the most popular Toyoda loom. 'It was really just a way for Platt Bros. to keep the loom off the competitive market,' says a local historian today. But the price was £100,000. Sakichi died a year later, and the money for the patent rights became the seed money for what was to become the Toyota Motor Company.

CHAPTER TWO
CHALLENGE: BUILD A CAR

'Everyone should tackle some great project at least once in their life,' Sakichi Toyoda told his son Kiichiro. 'I devoted most of my life to inventing new kinds of looms. Now it's your turn. You should make an effort to complete something that will benefit society.'

Kiichiro knew what that something should be. He had discussed it with his father often, but turning that dream of a domestic Japanese car into reality was to embark on a road strewn with roadblocks and potholes. The road could not have been traversed without extraordinary effort and dedication, and a good deal of luck.

Although much has been made of the countrified roots of the Toyoda family and the principles of the companies they founded, they were a shrewd and canny lot. Sakichi, the inventor with dirt under his fingernails, sent Kiichiro to study mechanical engineering at prestigious Tokyo Imperial University. Kiichiro carried on in his father's rough-hewn footsteps, but with his head crammed with technology. He had been a sickly boy, who had practically grown up on the floor of his father's factory, but he was studious and serious-minded.

Engines were on everybody's mind in machine shops and engineering schools at the time. The First World War was raging in Europe, and the Japanese military was growing – Japan was on the Allied side then – and mechanization was what modern Japan craved. After graduation Kiichiro joined his sister Aiko and her husband Risaburo on a visit to textile mills in Europe and the United States in 1921. Risaburo was an overseas representative of the C. Itoh trading company when he was introduced to Aiko Toyoda. When the couple married he was formally adopted into the Toyoda family and became influential in Toyoda family business ventures, alongside Sakichi and Sakichi's brothers, Heikichi and Sasuke.

It is said that it was during that early trip, seeing the ubiquity and utility of automobiles in countries beyond two vast oceans, that Kiichiro was struck with the full realization of the exciting challenge before him. Engines had intrigued him from the time his father built a small one and mounted it on a bicycle. Kiichiro got a better look at the world of automobiles in 1929 when he went back to England, this time with Mitsui & Co. representatives, to conclude the licensing of the Toyoda G-type automatic loom patents with Platt Bros. While the tedious, time-consuming final negotiations took place between Mitsui and Platt, he spent his time calling on auto plants in England, and again in the United States on his way home. He took voluminous notes on what he had seen and heard.

The auto business in Japan at the time had been virtually monopolized by Ford and General Motors after the Great Kanto Earthquake of 1923. Ford, which had sold those initial 800 Model T chassis that eventually became buses, hastened to build an assembly plant in Yokohama in 1925. Production rose quickly to 8,000 cars a year, all assembled from knockdown kits shipped from the US. General Motors followed in 1927 and upped the ante. Its Osaka plant could produce 10,000 cars a year. Ford bought enough land to expand, but was never able to do so. In fact Ford didn't sell its Yokohama land until, in the early 1980s, it was really obvious they were never going to build in Japan again.

Automobile fever had struck the nation. But, as they say in Detroit, to the dismay of car salesmen, the hard part of the business isn't selling them, it's making them. It is a costly business which requires a lot of money and a dizzying range of technologies that few enterprises can afford to employ. As in the United States, whose industry at one time boasted literally hundreds of automobile makers but was fast shrinking to a few hearty survivors, in Japan the weak, the faint of heart and the bankrupt were falling by the wayside. From as many as eighty makers, three companies more or less survived by the time Kiichiro returned from his trip, and together they managed to produce 436 hand-built vehicles in 1929. Still others were trying to enter the market.

It wasn't only a matter of talent and economics. Government officials grew more and more concerned about the balance of payments situation as Ford and GM imports of kits and subsequent sales soared. The Ministry of Commerce and Industry appointed a committee to look into the ways the government could promote a domestic industry. It began by setting some standards and then prompted the three companies to work together to design and produce the prototype of a Japanese standard truck and bus chassis. The job was completed in 1932, when the platform was unveiled. Encouraged by this development, several large conglomerate groups decided to give the business a try.

In a very real way Kiichiro Toyoda had an advantage over some of the others in the business. He knew that building an engine was the heart and soul of the effort to produce a car. His studies had taught him that the metals needed, and their quality, was key. Japanese companies would have to learn how to make those metals or he would have to import them until they learned how. If he did not wish to rely on foreign parts he would have to figure out how to make them himself and to encourage other Japanese firms to make them for him. This meant he would have to perfect methods of casting, forging and machining the hundreds, indeed thousands, of metal parts that went into a car, including the screws and fasteners. Wood and leather would not long suffice for car bodies, which meant that high-quality ductile sheet steel would be needed.

Fortunately, Toyoda Automatic Loom Works had a wealth of knowledge about casting metal parts, machining metal to close tolerances, and even chrome-plating the intricate gears and fittings for its automatic looms. Nagoya was an industrial town, a centre of manufacturing and companies there were considered to be advanced in contemporary technologies. It was also famous for the precision works of the Owari wall clock, a market leader at the time.

There were some parts makers in business in Japan, supplying the fledgling car industry. Many of them were buying parts abroad and reverse-engineering them. And many didn't know what they were doing. Eiji Toyoda, now honorary chairman of the Toyota Motor Corporation, once visited a prospective supplier of precision meters, to find the workshop was located under a railroad overpass. The whole shop shook violently every time a train passed.

Toyota chairman Shoichiro Toyoda, Kiichiro's son, recalls his father as 'a genuine engineer'. He says, 'Kiichiro gave much thought to an issue rather than rely on intuition. He always liked to accumulate facts. Before he made the decision to make an automobile engine he made a small engine. The cylinder block was the most difficult thing to cast, so he gained a lot of experience in that area and, based on the confidence he then had, he went ahead.

'He also placed emphasis on researchers or professors at universities, as well as workers. For gear technology he went to Prof. Masao Naruse of Tohoku University, for engines and heat to Prof. Shiro Nukiyama, and for metals and materials to Prof. Tokushichi Mishima. Today we are continually receiving advice. Many students who studied under these professors have come to Toyota and continued their research at the company. It was a beneficial place for these students. These are people who have nourished Toyota.'

Kiichiro reached out to old college mentors for help in getting his project under way, including Kazuo Kumabe, a professor at University of Tokyo, as it is now called, who was a member of the Ministry of Commerce and Industry's motor vehicle promotion committee, heading its design team. Kiichiro set a stunning goal for his venture: to go head-on against the cars coming from Ford and General Motors, making cars rivalling the competition, perhaps even bigger cars than they were assembling in Japan. They would be made, according to one of the countless memos he was fond of writing, with a production system that 'will reflect the particular conditions in Japan'. This may have been the germination of the idea behind the production system that would eventually evolve to influence manufacturing around the world.

In 1933 Kiichiro felt he was ready to build cars and asked Risaburo Toyoda, who headed the family business, to call a meeting of the board of directors to approve his move to add an automobile department to the Toyoda Automatic Loom Works.

The company was ready to start. By midyear it had produced ten motorcycle engines. Kiichiro sought out yet more experts in technology, including a steel specialist named Benzo Fukada, who immediately began to create a steel mill to make the kinds of steel that were unavailable from other steel-makers. Risaburo Ohshima, who had negotiated with Platt Bros. and was still in England, bought machine tools from Germany. He would become general manager of the first plant. A specialist in casting, Takatoshi Kan, was hired to produce the first design of a prototype plant that would be able to convert to mass production. Ohshima was named manager.

Even with all the Japanese experts on hand, producing that first real automobile engine, patterned after a Chevrolet offering of the day, took a year of trial and error. The first triumph, in September 1934, was a hefty 3,389 cc six-cylinder in-line engine, the Type A, which could deliver, after much redesign of its combustion chambers, 65 horsepower. Many of its parts had been reverse-engineered from foreign parts, some improved upon. The building of the chassis and its rather crude suspension system, and the hammering out of the body panels, caused fewer, if not less worrisome, problems. By the early summer of 1935 Kiichiro and his crew could stand back and admire the Model A1 passenger car. It was a formidable sight to behold. Patterned after the new concept of streamlining and taking off from the generous rounded curves of De Soto, Hudson and Chrysler, it was a gleaming, sturdy beauty, with styling following worldwide trends away from angular to more sculptured lines.

But what the Japanese government wanted in 1935 for the continuing modernization of the country was not passenger cars for personal mobility. The power of the military was growing. There was turmoil in Asia: civil war erupted in China in 1927, and Japan invaded Manchuria in 1931 to set up the puppet state called Manchukuo. Manchuria, a further foothold on the mainland, was being commercialized and militarized (Korea was already a client state, annexed in 1910). In 1935 Mao Tse Tung began his Long March to the caves of Yenan, from which he would eventually proclaim China a Communist state. In a few years, Japanese would move on China and capture Shanghai and Peking. The Second World War was just over the horizon.

The Bill Concerning the Manufacture of Motor Vehicles passed the Diet (Japanese parliament) in 1935 and its message was clear. It wanted truck production. A similar attempt by the government in the First World War gave subsidies to companies who could provide trucks to the Japanese army. Then, three companies – the shipbuilder Ishikawajima, Tokyo Gas & Electric and a vehicle repair company called Kaishinsha – were authorized to build trucks but produced none beyond a few experimental models. They were not equipped for the job. Like later attempts by the government to control and coerce the motor industry of Japan, this plan had run into a brick wall. Government ministries would later learn that motor people would accept government aid and accede to firm government demands. However, they resented government 'guidance', with which they only go along under duress, as the nine auto makers did in the 1980s by agreeing to 'voluntary' restraints of exports to the US that were anything but voluntary.

The few Japanese-made trucks that the military shipped to Manchuria for use in its rough terrain were not rugged enough for transporting troops and equipment over the unpaved roads and through the dust and extremes of temperature of northern China. By August of 1935, in anticipation of what was to come, Kiichiro and his company produced their first truck, called the G-1. It used the Type A engine and the platform of the Model A1 car, with a double seat cab behind a split windscreen, and sported a simple, no-nonsense grille and a wooden truck bed. It looked like a truck, but it had been hurried through the process to meet a deadline.

The new automobile department of the Toyoda Automatic Loom Works was in a hurry to get its truck and car production on the record and recognized, so that when the Bill Concerning the Manufacture of Motor Vehicles was passed Toyoda would be counted as a manufacturer. If companies were to be selected to produce vehicles under the terms of the new law, Kiichiro wanted to make sure that Toyoda was on that list. As Eiji Toyoda recalls, 'He knew the prospective designated companies would be protected and nurtured under the new law. Although what Toyota really wanted was to make passenger cars, we put those [plans] aside.'

The first truck was an imposing machine but it was, of course, rushing into production in less than six months, and it was understandably full of bugs. Although Kiichiro had taken pains to make as many components as he and his colleagues could fashion, and buy the best he could find on the Japanese market, the parts were of uneven quality. In a continual effort to improve the quality, when a new and better part was made in-house or a better one found from an outside supplier, Kiichiro would destroy any stock of old and less reliable parts. Historian Kingo

Saito of the Toyota Commemorative Museum of Industry and Technology in Nagoya points out that one of the advantages of patterning the first engine after a Chevrolet engine of its day was that, if the worst came to the worst, one could always buy imported spare parts and they would function properly. The prototype was taken out for its road trial but a repair crew with spare parts was sent out with it and, sure enough, on that test run the drive shaft broke, and the official company history reports that the transmission and the steering system collapsed as well.

Despite the disappointing first trial, the Toyoda crew went back to the plant and the drawing-board, determined to produce better trucks. They managed to build about twenty more in the remainder of 1935 and their quality improved, if only marginally. With the optimistic opening of sales outlets in Nagoya and Tokyo, trucks were delivered gingerly to the dealers, often breaking down on the way. With truck production under way and improving, Kiichiro again turned his attention to perfecting a passenger car.

In Tokyo the increasingly demanding army was pressuring the government to expel Japan Ford and Japan GM but, fearing diplomatic repercussions from the US, the Cabinet refused. The regulations that were finally promulgated accomplished the same thing. The 1936 law required that any company producing more than 3,000 motor vehicles a year be licensed by the government. The catch was that only companies that were 50 per cent owned by Japanese nationals and with Japanese nationals on their boards could be granted a licence. The incentives for those companies that could qualify under these rules were generous. These included a five-year exemption from income taxes, local and business revenue taxes, and import duties on machinery, equipment and materials bought abroad. Further, the government eased other restrictions on issuance of shares and bonds, but it also gave itself the right to be involved in approving any merger attempts and to oversee the production of vehicles for the military.

Toyota, Nissan and Isuzu were the favoured companies given a monopoly on the market and, although Ford and GM were not officially shut down, taxes and duties on their imported parts and components were raised drastically. At the same time foreign-exchange regulations were tightened to the point where the foreign companies could no longer afford to pay for what they imported. Besides, they had both completed their small 3,000-vehicle quota early in the year and would be allowed to produce no more. The companies tried to continue with curtailed operations but by 1939, after both attempted unsuccessfully to merge with either Toyota or Nissan, they shut down their manufacturing operations. (In 1984 an executive of Ford Japan came across an agreement drawn up and signed in 1939 for a joint venture owned 30 per cent each by Toyota and Nissan and 40 per cent by Ford. Eiji Toyoda notes that he remembers wondering why Shoichi Saito, chairman of the Toyota Motor Corporation in the 1970s, had been sent to the US in 1939. He now suspects it had something to do with this agreement. Whether such an agreement, which would technically have met the 50 per cent Japanese ownership and board membership rule, would have been approved is problematical; in any case it was never executed.)

NEW CAR, NEW NAME

Kiichiro and his crew were diligently making progress on the much-needed dies for stamping-machines to fashion steel parts, including body panels. Before the end of 1936 the Model AA passenger car was introduced, looking a bit sleeker than the Model A1. Kiichiro decided that his car needed a new logotype. The Toyoda emblem affixed to the bonnet of the Model A1 was a chromed circle surrounding the Chinese characters for the name Toyoda. It was difficult to read, didn't have instant recognition.

Kiichiro wanted something less complicated and more appealing. Announcing that it was now in the business of making passenger cars, the company sponsored a contest for a new name. The winning entry was simplicity itself: Toyota, not Toyoda, written in *katakana* syllables usually used for pronouncing foreign words. Written thus, in left to right Western style, the revised name is written in eight strokes of the pen or pencil. Toyoda, written in *katakana*, requires ten. Since eight is considered an auspicious number in Japan, the new logo carried with it not only simplicity but an augury of future success. The difference in the spellings has led to some confusion. Toyoda enterprises, such as the spinning and weaving and the automatic loom businesses, retained their names, but the automobile company and some affiliated companies became Toyota companies. (Shoichiro Toyoda, discussing the name confusion, says that one Japanese executive, Sony's co-founder Akio Morita, suggested facetiously that the Toyota name is so famous now that the family should change its name to Toyota.)

By the end of 1936 the company had exploited its basic designs as many ways as Kiichiro and his crew could stretch them. They produced, in addition to the Model A1 and AA cars and the G1 truck, a Model AB Phaeton with a cloth top from the design of the Model AA car, and also a Model DA bus chassis. All the vehicles managed to make it over the Hakone pass, west of Tokyo for a Tokyo exhibition of Toyota offerings. It was at this exhibition that word came of Toyota's selection under the new law. Toyota was under way.

NOW BUILD A FACTORY

'We needed more land,' says Kiichiro's son Shoichiro, gazing out the window of Toyota headquarters at the city of buildings on the very land he spoke of. 'So we moved from Kariya to this place.' Being one of three makers selected to produce cars for a nation was heady stuff. Obviously a new factory would have to be built. Kariya was the home of the early loom activity, but the area was agricultural and there was no room for an automobile factory of the size Kiichiro envisioned. Land-poor Japan was not blessed with an abundance of open flat space, being almost 80 per cent mountainous.

They found the site near Nagoya at a place called Koromo. Shoichiro says his father knew the area and the unpaved roads that criss-crossed it. He had driven them with his father. 'My father bought an American car, a Packard, I believe. I often encouraged him to speed up when we were driving together. It could go up to 60 miles an hour.' The Koromo land his father had in mind, says Shoichiro, was ideal: 'It was not suitable for rice paddies, or for farming. There was an irrigation canal and, although it was (theoretically) possible to grow rice crops if watered properly from the canal, the land was not watered. This place was a wasteland.' Another factor in the decision was that the mayor of Koromo 'helped us to obtain the land at a bargain price. That is why there is a bust of the mayor and of my father in the middle of Toyota City.'

The company folklore has it that, at this crucial point, with a major automobile assembly plant to be built, Kiichiro wrote his instructions to Takatoshi Kan on a scrap of paper: 'Please construct a plant at Koromo capable of producing 500 passenger cars and 1,500 trucks a month.' But of course it wasn't that simple, as good a story as it was. Kiichiro was a stickler for detail and he knew what he wanted. He and Kan had discussed at great length what would be needed. And what wouldn't. Even that early in the company's history Kiichiro was wedded to the idea of just-in-time production. He wanted no gigantic warehouse for storing costly parts. His idea was also based on the theory and hope that, if he could produce his vehicles on order – and be paid for them – he could pay for his raw materials and parts as he went along, not engendering any stockpiling or warehousing costs.

The Toyota Motor Co. Ltd (TMC) was officially created in August 1937 with Risaburo Toyoda as its first president. The new Koromo plant (now called the *honsha* or headquarters plant), a sprawling grid of steel-frame saw-tooth buildings, rose rapidly on the plain that Kiichiro had bought and in November 1938 the new TMC, later to become the Toyota Motor Corporation, was ready for production. A lot had been learned through trial and error, particularly in training a workforce that had little or no experience with mechanical production, thanks to supervisors who were proud of their ability to put theory into practice. The new plant had conveyor lines and shops laid out according to Kiichiro's concept of multi-tasking machines and multi-skilled workers. It was that gem that challenges all involved in manufacturing, a greenfield plant. The lessons learned here would be translated into vaunted concepts, most of them, as Kiichiro himself often said, ideas that came naturally, from common sense. And also from the kind of thrifty, economical efficient (and some would say stingy) characteristics of the people from Aichi. But as they prepared for an uncertain future the cauldron of war was brewing darker and darker in Asia as Japan's militarists made their drive for hegemony. The new Toyota Motor Company would soon be severely tested.

THE NEPHEW

In 1936, as Toyota Motor exported its first four hand-made trucks to Manchukuo, Eiji Toyoda, son of Sakichi's brother Heikichi, graduated from Tokyo Imperial University with a degree in mechanical engineering. It was a sort of triumph for him, as there had been some discussion as to whether the rather frail youth should even go to high school, let alone the university.

As Eiji tells it in his memoirs, Sakichi, the eldest in the Toyoda family, was ill when a family council was held on the subject of Eiji's higher education. It was the custom for the eldest to make weighty decisions and, as the second son, Eiji's father had to play a secondary role. Kiichiro had convinced his father to let him go to what is now University of Tokyo and had had to drop out for a year because of illness. Now, with the thought of Eiji going off, there was trepidation. Eiji, who was to become president of Toyota for fifteen years, was an adventurous young man, not greatly given to studying but keen on mah-jongg and sports he could practise without a partner, such as gymnastics. He was also the apple of Sakichi's eye.

As Eiji explained to me in Toyota City recently, 'Since Kiichiro was the only son of Sakichi and there was ten years' difference in age between Kiichiro and me, Sakichi treated me almost like his real son.' As Eiji's father was busy running the weaving and loom business, the family was housed in a corner of the factory site in Nagoya. Eiji was pressed into service frequently as a teenager to take down telephoned textile market quotations from the brokers. His father threw challenges at him to figure out what the fluctuating prices would mean to profitability, and so, as he put it, 'the mill served as a place of learning as well as a playground for me'. He lived there until he graduated from high school at the age of nineteen. (It is worth noting that under the Japanese system the final year of high school is equivalent to the first year of college in the United States.)

Sakichi took Eiji with him on business excursions and recreational trips. He built huge kites and would bring the boy with him to fly them. 'Fly a huge kite in the green windy hills in May and it makes a great roaring sound,' wrote Eiji a few years ago. 'I can still picture him taking in the string while looking up at his kite.'

Sakichi also took Eiji on the boy's first overseas trip. Sakichi had set up a spinning and weaving operation in Shanghai and during a summer vacation he made a visit to see to the completion of the plant. The boy's eyes were opened to a new vista of travel and of things foreign. Eiji relates that he was introduced into the curious world of foreign exchange by his Uncle Sakichi when he learned in China that some days the 10 yen coins he was given were worth only 9 sen, and some days 11 sen. The family businesses in modern times would learn that currency fluctuations often made the difference between profit and loss. Eiji remembers his uncle fondly: 'He was tall for a Japanese,' he says, 'or at least he seemed tall for us, but he did not pass the physical for the draft so maybe he wasn't tall enough for that. My father was very short so there was a difference between the two. He liked drinking and my father did too. And when they got together talking the room would fill with smoke.' Toyota historian Saito says Sakichi was a chain smoker who saved on expensive matches by keeping his *hibachi* charcoal burning.

In his final year at University of Tokyo Eiji designed a diesel engine for his thesis and graduated with an engineering degree. He declined becoming a civil servant and thought he might take some time off to consider his future employment. His father assumed that he would join the textile and loom businesses and work with him, but cousin Kiichiro stepped in and claimed Eiji for the automobile business. Kiichiro moved to Tokyo, where his son Shoichiro went to school (though Shoichiro would eventually go to university at Nagoya).

As for Eiji, he got no post-graduate respite from work. Kiichiro ordered him to set up a research lab in Tokyo, where Toyota had a partnership in a 'car hotel', one of the fireproof buildings required for housing automobiles after the devastating fires of the 1923 earthquake. As far as R&D goes it wasn't much of a lab, but Eiji cleaned it up and made the most of it. His orders were general, and they included inspecting the many vehicles that were brought to the car hotel for repair. Kiichiro seemed interested in the cutting-edge technology of the time and he instructed Eiji to learn about the autogiro, forerunner of the helicopter, and about rockets. Nothing came of either research project, but Eiji ingested all the available written material on both subjects. Kiichiro also used the lab to bring more technical experts into the company. The first was a specialist in thermodynamics, Prof. Hanji Umehara, a lecturer at Tohoku University, who was asked to help supplier companies make better radiators for Kiichiro's troublesome engines, which were prone to overheating. When a former classmate, Kazuo Kumabe, told Kiichiro he was taking a trip to Europe, Kiichiro asked him to bring back any interesting cars he saw. Kumabe bought a front drive DKW in Germany and, said Eiji, 'After driving it around for a while we took it apart, then proceeded to test-build several cars based on it.' The test-built cars were completed two years later, powered by two-cycle, two-cylinder engines. 'It was the first time,' wrote Eiji, 'that drawings I made were transformed into a real car.'

A crucial mission assigned to the young Eiji was the search for reliable parts suppliers. 'Without the parts you needed, things never went the way they were supposed to,' he wrote in his memoirs. Finding good suppliers would be crucial to the operation of the new plant. Kiichiro kept in touch with the operation of the plant daily by telephone, and after a time decided to transfer Eiji to a new division at Kariya he would call the Total Vehicle Engineering Administration Department, of which he was the only employee. He had barely begun his work there when Japanese and Chinese soldiers clashed at the Marco Polo Bridge in west Peking in July 1937. The Sino-Japanese war was sparked by the incident, and a month later Eiji was drafted. He spent two months caring for the horses and cleaning out the stables of a field artillery unit in Nagoya before he was released as an essential war worker to go back to Toyota Motor Company.

Candidly, Eiji admitted that for a time through early 1937 'we had been unable to sell the vehicles we made. One reason was the depressed economy but, more importantly, our product just couldn't pass muster.' It was one reason Kiichiro had sent him back to Kariya, to find out how to fix the problem of poor quality. He wrote of the dire situation, 'If we failed to act promptly and effectively the company would go under. It was as simple as that. Or so we thought. The situation changed abruptly when the war in China broke out and the army bought up all our trucks, cleaning out our entire stock. Military procurements for the war were what saved the company.'

CHAPTER THREE
WAR AND REBIRTH

If anyone in Japan had doubts about the outcome of the war against the United States it was people such as Kiichiro Toyoda, who had seen American industrial might first hand. It was not lost on him that Japan was producing six million tons of steel a year, which was the equivalent of twenty days' production in the US. And it was evident from the outset of the war that building vehicles was going to get increasingly difficult. From the first heady days of military victories abroad, supplies were short at home. Virtually everything needed to build with was considered strategic material, and as the days and months wore on commodities, including food, became scarce. For a country that lived on imported raw materials the situation grew more and more troubling. Defying wartime regulations, many companies, including Toyota, started to hoard precious supplies.

Even before the attack on Pearl Harbor, steel for truck makers was rationed and the supply of the many different types needed to build particular vehicles was not guaranteed. To solve the problem for the Toyota Motor Company (TMC), the Toyoda Automatic Loom Works expanded its in-house steel mill and a new company, the Toyoda Steel Works Ltd. was formed to produce speciality steels. Then TMC spun off its machine-tool-making division into another new company, the Toyoda Machine Works Ltd. The lab in Tokyo set about developing better, longer-lasting batteries for vehicles as the oil shipments into Japan dwindled under Allied submarine attacks on the tankers.

At the new TMC plant manufacture was at best sporadic. The flow of materials was so inconsistent that production limped along. Wrote Eiji of that period: 'We'd get orders from the military telling us to make so many trucks that month. Since material allotments came from one place and production orders from another, there was no way we could use the just-in-time system that we had developed with such care and effort . . . Even with enough pig iron on hand for 10,000 trucks, if all you've got is 3,000 units' worth of sheet steel, you're only going to be able to turn out 3,000 vehicles.' Sometimes they would bargain for more pig iron than they were allotted which they might be able to trade for some sheet steel somewhere. 'Most of our energy went into finding the materials we needed rather than building vehicles,' wrote Eiji. The secret, jealously guarded stockpiles of materials held by many Japanese companies helps to explain the surprising ability of some companies to get back into production quickly after the war.

There were other headaches. The workforce was recruited from wherever available people could be found and was grossly inefficient. Eiji recalls that it included nuns and geishas 'and even convicted criminals'. The workers had to be housed in dormitories and fed despite dwindling food supplies. The government impressed millions into war service, including school-children. Eiji once vented his outrage that the convicts were required under the penal code to receive a specific food ration which was greater than the shared ration allotted the rest of the workers.

Despite production woes, in 1943 Toyota was ordered to develop aircraft engines, and a joint effort was mounted with the Kawasaki Aircraft Co. By the end of the war they had managed to produce only 151 engines. As shortages became more critical, the military considered ways to stretch its supply of strategic materials. One result was an order to Toyota to simplify its trucks. The amount of steel in the frames was reduced and, according to Eiji Toyoda's recollection: 'Toward the very end of the war we were told that one headlight was enough and that we didn't need to install brakes on all four wheels – brakes just on the back wheels would do.' In due course one truck headlight was affixed to a grille that consisted of a single vertical bar of steel. The half-installed brake job made the trucks 'downright dangerous', in Eiji Toyoda's opinion.

Some ingenious vehicles were devised, though. They included a small truck that could be disassembled and carried in pieces by a number of soldiers through the rough terrain of far-flung places such as New Guinea and assembled later on more suitable ground. Toyota also built 198 lumbering amphibious four-wheel-drive vehicles and tested the prototype on Tokyo's Sumida River. Then came a desperate flotilla of unmanned plywood *kamikaze* boats loaded with explosives, designed to be sent against enemy ships. The small boats ran on truck engines but, as Eiji points out, if they bumped into a log or some other obstruction in the water on the way to the target, they would shatter. These last-ditch kinds of weapons were a sign of the military's desperation, as its fast-dwindling manpower was stretched across Asia and military hardware production on the home front was not only inadequate but could no longer be delivered to the faraway battlefields.

Although Nagoya and its clustered wartime aircraft plants and machine shops was a 'target rich' city for American bombers, for some reason the new Toyota plant in Koromo did not seem to be considered vital enough to Japan's war effort to be assigned for attack. Or so the staff at Toyota thought. There had been several aerial strafing raids, but no serious damage. And then, on 14 August 1945, the day before Japan surrendered, three B-29s appeared overhead and each dropped a large conventional bomb.

Shoichiro Toyoda was on summer vacation from Nagoya University and was working as a trainee at TMC. He remembers the air-raid siren sounding often and workers scurrying to shelter. Usually the planes ignored Koromo and concentrated on Nagoya. The clouds of smoke from the destruction in Nagoya were clearly visible from as far away as Koromo. Shoichiro was not at the plant when the bomb fell, but when he got there it looked to him as though there had been a great deal of damage. 'The bomb blast was very strong and all the slates from the roofs near by were blown away. So at a glance it appeared like an enormous amount of damage, but actually it was not that big. All the people managed to evacuate, so there were no casualties. After the bombing, workers set about clearing the broken tiles and trying to repair the damage.'

The next day, 15 August 1945, the reedy voice of Emperor Hirohito was broadcast to the stunned nation. His voice had never been broadcast before and he spoke in obscure courtly language. The precise words he spoke were not understood by all who heard, but his meaning was soon clear to everyone. The war was over. Japan would have to 'endure the unendurable' and accept the Allied surrender terms.

Says Shoichiro Toyoda, 'We were disappointed when we heard the news declaring the end of the war. But Hisayoshi Akai, a Toyota vice-president, said with a lively voice that days of freedom had finally arrived.' Many of the workers couldn't believe what had happened. Some wept at their machines, and some of the young students who had been mobilized for war work lined up and marched back to the dormitories, where a company official later found them on their beds, sobbing. The highly censored Japanese news media had not prepared the nation for defeat, even though it was obvious the war was being lost as American bombers flattened Japan's cities virtually unopposed. Even the nature of the atomic bombing of Hiroshima and Nagasaki on 6 and 8 August was not clearly revealed to the public.

At Koromo nobody knew what to do. The drafted workers, more than 9,000 of them, wanted to go home and, as there was little transportation and hardly any money, a plan was devised to start sending groups of them home. Those helping out the resettling of the workers were busy, Eiji remembers, 'but the rest of us didn't quite know what to do with ourselves. We came to the office out of force of habit but instead of working we just sat around blankly, asking each other what would happen when the American troops arrived.'

The first Americans to arrive were members of a bombing survey team who showed up to check the results of the bombing. They had aerial photos of the damage. Eiji says it was by talking with these Americans that he realized for the first time that Toyota had been targeted and that they had not been hit by mistake or randomly: 'I was horrified when I took a look at the bombing schedule the commission had with them. Toyota was to have been bombed and burned to the ground exactly one week later, on 21 August.'

Vice-president Akai gathered the managers and gave them a pep talk. He tried to encourage them by saying Toyota had a role to play in rebuilding Japan. Within a few days most of the workers outside the plant's 2,700-strong regular workforce had gone home. As far as Kiichiro and his staff knew, they were out of business, at least for the time being and maybe for ever. His grand plan to build automobiles had been dashed by Japanese military and political adventurism. In that last year of the war, the plant he envisioned producing 1,500 trucks and 500 passenger cars each month had made a grand total of 3,275 trucks and buses, and not a single passenger car.

STARTING AGAIN

The future was unpredictable, but the remaining employees were put to work immediately planting vegetables in the infertile soil at Koromo. A flour mill, bakery and charcoal plant were built on the premises. Kiichiro ordered Eiji to set up a chinaware business with ceramics makers in the area, and he sent Shoichiro off to the northernmost tip of Japan's northern main island of

Hokkaido to learn everything he could about making fish paste, a staple of the Japanese diet. Other Toyoda companies began producing goods such as pots and pans. As luck would have it, the Occupation authorities, realizing the need for trucks in rebuilding the destroyed infrastructure of the nation, permitted TMC to start building trucks again. By the end of September it was able to produce eighty-two trucks.

At this uncertain juncture, Kiichiro reached for his pen and put his thoughts about the future into a timely and remarkably cogent memo: 'We have finally come to the point where Japan will have to convert to a free-market economy like that of the United States and compete with the rest of the world on an equal basis. We must, therefore, reform our protected and monopolistic companies.

'The Japanese auto industry has been fostered and protected in a controlled economy and has never braved the rough waves of a free-market system. It is like a hothouse plant. Moreover, viewed impartially from a global standpoint, Toyota is far from being a first-class company. Because of Japan's defeat in the war, we should see ourselves as something like a third-class auto company.

'We will find it difficult to hold a clear course without foundering in the stormy seas of a free-market economy. The ability of this company, which has sustained heavy blows, to make the transition from a controlled to a free-market economy will determine its ultimate success or failure. However, if we can succeed in a free-market economy we will have a bright future ahead of us. Everything depends on our own determination.'

Having said that, he proceeded to reorganize the company and its group. He and Shotaro Kamiya resurrected the dealer network, brought the dealers to Koromo for a conference and put across the inspirational message. They also managed to win over some Nissan dealers, although Tokyo and Osaka remained favourite Nissan territory: their dealers outnumbered Toyota's only in those two cities. Still uncertain what the Occupation would require – it was possible that plant and equipment could be seized and shipped off to another country as war reparations – Kiichiro forged ahead with plans for a new, roomy small car. By January 1947, Kiichiro's staff had produced a small prototype Model SA passenger car with a 995 cc engine that delivered 27 horsepower. They named it Toyopet. Then the General Headquarters of the Occupation, usually referred to as GHQ, began ordering cars: it wanted fifty large cars from Toyota for its own use, and authorized the other auto makers to produce as many as 300 cars under 1,500 cc. Nissan produced its Datsuns under this order.

THE TROUBLE WITH MONEY

The nation was recovering slowly under Occupation policies, and Toyota was able to produce cars, but inflation was rampant. Money was becoming worthless and difficult to get at that. As Eiji Toyoda puts it, 'We did not have a problem selling, but it was difficult to collect payment.' Toyota began asking for a large down payment, as much as half the selling price, on every truck ordered, a necessary move that discouraged sales. The cash flow situation was horrendous. At one point in 1948 the company's debt exceeded its capital by eight times.

GHQ sought to cope with the nation's economic woes by calling in Detroit banker Joseph Dodge. His solution was to institute a stringent tight monetary policy that became known as the Dodge Line. It became virtually impossible to borrow funds, and for Toyota, deeply in debt, it meant that plans would have to be cut drastically. By the middle of 1949 expansion plans were shelved. Managers had already taken voluntary pay cuts. After much negotiation the employees agreed to a 10 per cent wage cut and as a part of the deal the company promised its union that it would not fire anyone, which had been Kiichiro's policy. But the pay cuts didn't help, and Kiichiro and his bankers saw that a reduction in the payroll was necessary, despite earlier promises and a signed company pledge. He asked for 1,600 workers to retire from the company voluntarily. That sparked a series of work stoppages and demonstrations that lasted over two agonizing months. Eiji remembers being confronted by 2,000 angry workers 'filled with hostility toward me'. Labour turmoil was breaking out all around Japan. Nissan and other auto companies would undergo testing times with their unions before the workforce was calmed and a less politicized system was instituted in the form of company-wide unions.

To compound the matter, soon the banks threatened to stop the money flow. The company was headed for bankruptcy. At the height of the impasse, Kiichiro Toyoda made a fateful decision: he would resign as president. It was a particularly Japanese way of settling a dispute, or at least calming it. By resigning from the company he created he would accept responsibility for the troubles which, of course, were beyond his personal control. Eventually more employees volunteered to leave than had been asked for, and the company sought to find jobs for them at other companies. Labour peace was restored.

The consortium of banks that was financing Toyota demanded as part of the rescue package that the sales side be separated from the manufacturing side, and a new company, the Toyota Motor Sales Company (TMS), was founded, which would have no direct financial connection with the Toyota Motor Company. The banks wanted more transparency in the operation. They wanted assurances that the cars TMC built could be sold by TMS. The sales company also could aid TMC's product planning by suggesting what kinds of cars it should make for TMS to sell.

DIVINE AID

Eiji Toyoda entered the 1950s with a long trip to the United States that convinced him the company could eventually compete with the American car makers. He stayed in the US for three and a half months, hoping to learn what he could about modern American production methods. During his six weeks in Detroit he was treated cordially by the then new chairman, the youthful Henry Ford II, and other Ford executives. 'They were very kind to me,' recalls Eiji. 'They even treated me to meals every day; back then we did not have much money, and there was a limit to how much we were allowed to take out of Japan on visits to foreign countries. I had only $3,000 to cover all the expenses, including the air fare to the States.'

All the auto companies were open to the visitor – who would ever have thought in 1950 that a Japanese car maker would ever be a threat to the Big Three? 'They let me see every step of production operations,' says Eiji now. 'The knowledge I acquired was very useful. But, at the time, Toyota was producing forty cars a day, and Ford was making 8,000 units. That was a 200 times difference. Because the gap was so enormous, although I found the knowledge useful, it was not possible to apply the methods right away.' He brought away a few ideas, including that for Toyota's first suggestion system programme.

At Ford, Eiji listened in on meetings on quality control and budgetary management. He attended lectures and joined in hands-on work with the newest automatic transmissions in workshops for dealership servicemen. He wandered around the highly integrated River Rouge plant, visited the historic Highland Park plant where Henry Ford built the Model T, inspected a carburettor plant, and a bearing plant, and even toured the auto and truck assembly plants of the Chrysler Corporation. He didn't get a chance to visit General Motors but he remembers thinking on leaving Detroit that he hadn't seen anything that was beyond Toyota's ability. He also travelled to Cleveland and points east, visiting supplier plants and machine tool plants all through the north-east of America. With little money to spend, on weekends he visited art museums, and in New York walked in Central Park and rode the subway lines to their end. During the week he would strike out by train or bus to visit more plants.

When the Korean War broke out in June 1950, Shotaro Kamiya of TMS was also in the United States hoping to make some sort of sales arrangement with Ford. Nothing came of it as Ford found itself deluged with emergency Defense Department work for the Korean conflict. When Kamiya returned to Japan empty-handed and depressed, he found the company was suddenly flush with orders. In July the US Defense Department put in an order for 1,000 trucks. By March 1951, TMS would have orders totalling nearly 5,000. These procurement orders were the answer to Toyota's reconstruction prayers. Eiji called them a gift from heaven. Kamiya said they were Toyota's 'salvation'. The initial orders enabled Toyota to pay a dividend for the first time in seven years.

By 1956 the Occupation and the Korean War were both history but the Cold War was on and Japan was now an ally. The Pentagon's procurement from Japan, including vehicles, equipment and services of all kinds, totalled almost $2 billion. Naoto Ichimanda, the governor of the Bank of Japan, called US procurement 'divine aid'.

With the picture thus brightening the management team approached Kiichiro and asked him to come back and take over the reins of the company. He was reluctant. He complained that the company was only building trucks and he had devoted his life to the goal of building passenger cars, but president Taizo Ishida finally persuaded him. Only weeks later, and before he could take over, Kiichiro Toyoda suffered a fatal stroke. He was fifty-seven years old. Less than three months later Risaburo

Toyoda was on his sickbed and urged Eiji Toyoda to start making passenger cars. Eiji assured him that plans were under way for auto production. Risaburo never recovered from his illness and died in June at the age of sixty-eight.

On New Year's Day, 1955, Eiji Toyoda put on his tuxedo, slipped behind the wheel of Toyota's first post-war production passenger car, the Crown, and drove it off the assembly line. The Crown would soon be heading for the US and the beginning of a new era in the world's automotive history.

CHAPTER FOUR
ENTER OHNO

He terrified everybody who worked for him, drove them un-
mercifully, gave them impossible assignments, criticized them,
belittled them, threw things at them, kicked them. Some assigned
to work with him did their best to avoid him. But he got their
attention and taught them a lot. His teaching reverberated around
the industrial world as he redefined and reorganized how modern
factories work. His systematic analysis and restructuring of the
way cars are made became known as the Toyota Production
System (TPS), which made his company 'the machine that
changed the world'. It is generally referred to as Lean Manufacturing or Lean Production.

Despite the accolades thrown his way Taiichi Ohno was not
vain about his ideas. He did not seek extraordinary credit for
inventing the system, and in fact he credited the basic thinking
to Sakichi and Kiichiro Toyoda. The young men he taught,
many of them now high-ranking executives at Toyota, admit to
being proud to have taken his abuse, and take a perverse pleasure
in telling stories of Ohno's drastic teaching methods. 'At first
there was a lot of resistance both from within the organization
and from outside,' says Fujio Cho, an executive vice-president
who worked with Ohno for fifteen years. 'What he was trying
to do was very drastic, a completely new way of doing things,
and in the initial stages there was nobody who was willing to
cooperate with him. However, he was the type of person who
would never give up. Until he died he continued to work on
the system he created.' Cho remembers Ohno prowling the shop
floor watching and asking questions. 'He repeatedly asked the
question "Why?" until he was satisfied with the answer and the

person he was interrogating got the point of it. He kept asking the same questions over and over.' In fact, a part of Ohno's technique was to ask why five times, each time hoping to get closer to the problem. As he described it, if you asked why the machine stopped and the answer was that there was an overload and a fuse blew, the next question should be why was there an overload? If that answer was that the bearing wasn't properly lubricated and it seized, then why wasn't it properly lubricated, and if the pump was not working sufficiently to lubricate it, why wasn't it? And eventually, after asking five exasperating whys the root of the problem might be identified, along with many mistakes or contributing factors along the way. His reasoning was that, until you found the root cause of a difficulty, you might waste your time with fixes that do not solve the basic problem. 'His idea was not to sit at a desk and theorize without seeing for himself exactly how the work was being done,' says Cho.

Nampachi Hayashi is a specialist in TPS, and a survivor of the Ohno school. He says at first he tried to avoid being around Ohno. 'At that time I was scared and I was so upset that I couldn't sleep at night. He was very tall, and short-tempered. He kicked things and people, and he even threw things at us. Every time he acted that way we tried to correct the way we were doing things. Then he gave a very good explanation of why he had to scold us. I think in the process he tried to persuade us that to implement a new system we needed to change our way of thinking 180 degrees. Every time we tried to justify our behaviour by making excuses he scolded us.' Hayashi says Ohno was making examples of his staff members so they would transmit Ohno's ideas to others. He wanted to keep everybody focused on the root problem.

At one point Hayashi was dispatched to the paint shop to look into the quality problem there. 'We were having to repaint two or three units out of ten. I was there to make corrections.' The company was still in its infancy and everybody was just learning.

Hayashi noticed that the workers were having difficulty moving the car bodies into the repaint shop, 'so I attached a simple motor to the conveyor system for the repaint shop, making it easier to move the bodies. But when Mr Ohno saw it he was furious.'

'I was dumbfounded,' says Hayashi. 'I didn't know why he was so angry because I thought I had done a good thing for the workers and I tried to justify my position. After all, I said, it was *kaizen*, an improvement.' But his *kaizen* only made it easier to repaint botched paint jobs when he had been sent to troubleshoot the problem of the bad paint jobs themselves and eliminate the need to repaint the bodies.

Ohno ordered Hayashi to detach the motor from the conveyor system and snapped at the embarrassed and humiliated subordinate, 'If you think the workers are in trouble then you, yourself, push those bodies.' Ohno walked away. 'For half a day I pushed those bodies myself,' Hayashi remembers. 'And then Mr Ohno came back and said "You are an engineer, so your responsibility is to create a system so that no failures occur, that no rejects will be made. *That* is your job." To fix the paint problem was my job, not to distract myself with the conveyor system.'

A colleague of Hayashi, now a senior managing director of the corporation, had an even more humiliating but illuminating object lesson taught to him by Ohno. Working on the body shop welding line one day he noted that a nut was broken from the frame he was welding. Ohno told him to find the nut and not to do anything else until he found it. 'He spent three days trying to find the nut. All he did every day was search for it, until he finally found it. Ohno made him find the nut because he wanted him to understand why the incident happened. If you don't know at what point the nut fell off you can't come up with a corrective measure to avoid the problem in the future.'

Ohno didn't stand over everybody all the time, but to some it seemed like this evil genius was always aware of what they were doing. Hayashi has another incident imprinted indelibly on his memory: 'I was on the assembly line, watching the process of tightening nuts on muffler insulators. Every time the worker tried to affix the insulator, he had trouble making the bolt line up properly with the drilled hole, so he was stopping the line frequently. Too frequently, I thought, and I made a move to call the general manager about the part that didn't fit properly. But Ohno was there, and he barked, "Don't try to escape from here!" I saw that I had to solve this problem immediately or he would not go away. So I looked at the problem carefully, found the misalignment, and was about to go to the sampling plant to make the corrections on the plate when Mr Ohno said again, "Don't try to escape!" I had nothing to do but stand there and watch the line, and he again shouted, "What are you doing?" ' Hayashi was doing nothing, and he suddenly realized it. So he moved to the line and worked with the assembler until they came up with a way to attach the plate satisfactorily, even with the slight misalignment. Still Ohno kept watching. The worker was able to do the job without stopping the line, 'So the problem was solved and no more problems came up so I was relieved, when Mr Ohno shouted again, "You should immediately run to the stamping line and make a correction on the hole location." ' When Hayashi returned Ohno was gone.

The object lesson of the day was that that, if Hayashi had gone to the stamping plant immediately, the problems on the assembly line would have continued, 'so the first thing to do was make corrections on the line, even though it was not a perfect solution. I thought, well, I am not a fool and if he had explained it I would have understood it, but I was told that if I was reprimanded this way I would never make the mistake again in other circumstances.'

GETTING LEAN

It is an article of faith in manufacturing today that warehouses full of inventory are anathema to lean and profitable production. But when Toshio Mizushima, who is now president of Toyota Motor Manufacturing (UK) Ltd., was in charge of the press shop at Toyota's Motomachi plant the system was not yet in effect. Or so Mizushima thought: 'We wanted to produce more press panels and so to increase our production volume we needed more stores. We wanted to rent another warehouse and Mr Ohno refused. Instead, his staff came to our plant to reduce our die-changing time.'

In the middle 1960s, it still took on average two hours to change the heavy contoured dies in the giant presses that stamp out parts. On some lines, it took as long as four or even eight hours to remove the large and heavy dies with cranes, then set a new die carefully in perfect alignment into the press and set it up with precision so a run of perfect parts was possible. As this was such tedious, time-consuming work, the shop philosophy almost everywhere was to use the existing dies as long as possible and stamp out enough parts to last for quite a while. In this case, they were running lot sizes large enough for at least a half-month's production.

Ohno abruptly and alarmingly slashed the lot size in half. 'That meant we had to change the dies more frequently,' says Mizushima. 'So we worked overtime, Saturdays and Sundays, to do it.' It suddenly dawned on everybody that 'to survive we must reduce our die-changing time. Everyone concentrated on this. It took us more than six months, maybe a year, but finally we achieved a single die change in less than ten minutes.

'What we learned is that while we improved we created the means for improvement. When he cut the lot size everybody had to improve, otherwise we couldn't survive,' says Mizushima.

It also created crews of skilled die setters, forced them to become better skilled, to use jigs, to invent equipment and make it standard so that their work was sure, fast and repeatable. Merely changing the dies is simple, hard work. It is locating them precisely and making the fine adjustments needed to turn out perfectly fitting parts that is difficult and has to be mastered. Toyota became the industry's leader in fast die changing time. In Detroit, at the same period, it was customary to shut down plants while long weeks were set aside to change the dies. Tales of Toyota's fast changing times were viewed with scepticism in Detroit at first. Detroit, however, was wedded to a system of large-scale production and naturally needed bigger lot sizes. Toyota was making smaller numbers of cars and models on cramped lines and found, through Ohno, the way to produce the parts needed 'just in time' to go on to the cars on the line. This allowed money-saving minimum inventories and improved efficiency.

Cho, who much later carried his experience in the TPS with him to Kentucky as the president of the new plant, Toyota Motor Manufacturing Kentucky, Inc. (TMMK), says that, despite the horror stories of Ohno's behaviour, when he was not on the job 'Ohno was a true gentleman. Even on the golf course he never got in somebody else's way and he was always concerned about others.' But Cho admits with a grin that 'when it came to the job he was very frightening to other people'. Ohno does not come off in anybody's reminiscences as a warm and cuddly guy; rather, he was in the mould of a didactic, harsh, authoritarian schoolmaster so common in Japan during his time.

'It was his creed that the top priority was to eliminate all waste, and by waste he meant anything that was unnecessary at that moment, be it goods or action. He was trying to make himself hate any form of waste, and he thought when he became unable to find or detect any waste in the company it would be the time for him to quit.'

He also defined a machine breakdown or a defective product

as waste. Says Cho, 'He told us that machinery, if it is maintained properly on a regular basis, will work fine for a long time, and that if a machine breaks down it is usually because a human broke it by not maintaining it properly.'

Hayashi admits that, in training employees, 'I am not as scary as Mr Ohno, but I do try to use his methods to train young people. However, since Japan has developed and become a rich country, if we applied Mr Ohno's exact technique it would not work. I do, however, understand that explaining things first doesn't make people feel the experience as vividly in the mind.' Hard object lessons were considered part of the discipline of life in Japan, perhaps the secular equivalent of the Zen *koan*, 'What is the sound of one hand clapping?' In one instance Ohno brought one of his protégés to a supplier factory and showed him an operation on a car body that was being handled by ten men. Ohno told him, 'This job can be done by five men. I'll be back Friday.' He turned on his heel and disappeared, leaving the young man with his mouth agape and his mind reeling. He was expected to redesign the work for only half the manpower, with no other instructions. First he had to understand just what all these people were doing and why they were doing it. Then he had to figure out the streamlining of the operation. After a week of sleepless nights he devised a five-man reduction. Ohno returned on Friday as threatened, and his student explained the revised process to him, and how the extra five men could be reassigned to other jobs. Ohno grunted by way of congratulations and walked away.

Fujio Cho points out that this kind of 'tough love' nurturing of subordinates 'is a natural way of life in Japan'. The Western way is different, though. In the US, while training team members at the then new Kentucky plant, he noted that the boss would watch an employee doing a job and wait until he finished the work before criticizing or correcting him. 'In my view you should monitor and interrupt him as he is doing the work and give him instructions as necessary. But that concept didn't seem to work in the American environment. So I asked, "Why do you wait for the result? Why not interrupt in the process and correct a bad habit?" The answer was, "The people here are professionals in their own fields and we can't look over other people's shoulders and get in the way." I thought, well, yes, this is true, these American people are experts in their own fields, and they have their pride in what they are doing, so I should respect their pride, professionalism and expertise and not interrupt. But once that work is completed, 100 per cent of the responsibility rests with the person who did the work.'

However, he says, 'In the Japanese way of doing things the boss will interrupt in in the middle of the process and give advice. He might say, "You should do it this way or that way," so when the process is completed and if the result is not good, or the quality is not good, it will be difficult to make the person take 100 per cent of the responsibility.' On reflection, Cho says, 'The Japanese system is based, after all, on generalists, not specialists. People learn how to do things after they enter a company, and there are advantages to that system. But I was very much impressed in the US by the way they gather professionals to create a team, assign responsibilities and roles to each person and each works individually but with a team strategy. That was very impressive to me. And it would be very difficult to do something similar in Japan.'

THE SYSTEM

In 1937 Taiichi Ohno was a mechanical engineer working at Toyoda Spinning and Weaving when he heard talk about the productivity of foreign workers being higher than that of the Japanese. If the disparity was as large as said, as much as nine or ten to one, then the Japanese were clearly doing something

1 Sakichi Toyoda (1867–1930), innovator of modern textile-making machinery, and founder of a giant industrial enterprise. He urged his son, Kiichiro Toyoda, to build automobiles 'with Japanese hands'.

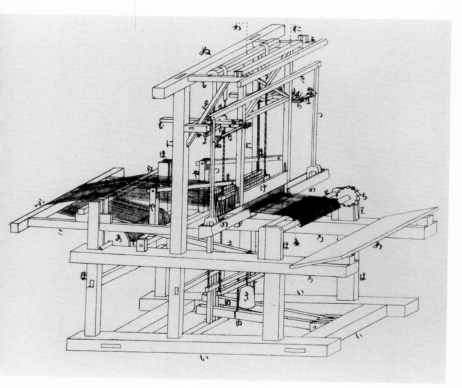

2 Schematic sketch of Sakichi Toyoda's first invention, an automatic handloom built of wood. It was the first of many designs that made the Toyoda's companies successful in the textile world, as this was the first of its kind to allow a single operator to monitor several looms simultaneously.

3 Kiichiro Toyoda (1894–1952), founder of Toyota Motor Company. He fulfilled his father's plea to build 'made in Japan' automobiles by creating Toyota Motor Company, Ltd.

4 The first prototype auto was the Model A1, completed in May 1935. Only a few crude copies were built for road testing while development work continued on cars for the market.

5 Prospective Toyota dealers gathered in 1936 to see a demonstration of the first car to carry the new Toyota emblem, the Model AA (two here flanking the dealers).

wrong, wasting effort, he reasoned. He pondered the question of productivity improvement for years. The system he devised is based on the total elimination of waste. The support for his concept is in just–in–time delivery of materials, and what he called autonomation, or 'automation with a human touch'.

To Ohno, just–in–time meant having the right parts needed in assembly reach the assembly line at the right place, at the time they are needed, and no more than are needed. The notion of autonomation came from the ingenuity of Sakichi Toyoda, whose machines caught the attention of foreign manufacturers because they were built with an internal tension device that shut the machine down when one of the threads broke. This enabled one worker to handle many machines and did away with the need for constant inspection of the weaving work of only a few machines. That was a major productivity improvement. He reasoned that such devices could be rigged to ordinary lathes and milling machines so that a worker could operate more than a single machine, as was then the case in most factories, and could probably even learn to operate several kinds of machines at the same time. He had noted that, in most cases, workers in single–skill jobs spent most of their time watching the machine doing the work and adding no value themselves.

Further, with machines designed to stop when there is an abnormality, the stopping itself draws attention to the process, and instead of quietly 'covering up' the problem, the stopping, Ohno said, 'forces awareness on everyone'. Today in Toyota plants a prominent illuminated signs called *andon* gives everybody in the plant a plethora of information, including updates on the current production rate and the status of systems in the plant. When the line is stopped the position of the stoppage is indicated on the *andon* – and a musical ditty, usually selected by the team members – plays. This alerts everyone, and team and group leaders, as necessary, rush to help solve whatever problem has developed.

49

Ohno pondered how to eliminate overproduction of parts to satisfy the needs of an assembly operation, and decided to turn the process around and look at the production flow in reverse. It became the heart of the new system. He took the final assembly line as the starting-point. Everything upstream, all the parts and materials needed for the final assembly, are provided just as the assembly process needs them and not before. His idea was to have the end process pull the parts through the system, rather than the standard system in which a flood of materials is prepared and on call for when or if needed and pushed into the system. When an assembler needed the next part he would go upstream and get it, rather than having it cascade down upon him. A system of small cards, called *kanban*, which means sign board, was devised to affix to small lot containers. When the first item from a container is empty the *kanban* is withdrawn and together with its mates is sent to the supplier, who then makes and replaces only the same number of containers of parts or pieces. It is shipped to the plant and put on the line at the proper place, which is indicated on the *kanban* card. This helps ensure a consistent, smooth and continuous flow of materials between suppliers and the factory. While the parts are being brought into the system and on line, the workers themselves could do the inspecting, eliminating the need for a separate category of inspectors. This is all much more difficult to do than to describe, for it requires precision.

When in 1943 Chuo Spinning Company was absorbed into Toyota Motor, Ohno went with it, although he was not an automobile expert. In fact he was the product of an industrial high school in Nagoya and went to work in the thread making division of Toyoda because his father knew Kiichiro. And so, without any automotive experience, he began to learn about the business and to analyse the processes, comparing them with what he knew of the textile plant. As head of the machine shop at Toyota's Koromo plant Ohno was able to try out his ideas, but slowly. The single-skilled craftsmen in the shops did not like his idea of grouping machines of different kinds in L-shapes or parallel to each other so that one individual could supervise the lot. It took years for Ohno to develop operators with a broad spectrum of production skills, even though Japanese unions were not organized into the detailed function orientation of US and European unions.

Ohno argued in his memoirs that the waste of overproduction is natural, especially in a society that has rural or agricultural roots, like most of Japan. He wrote that, before, during and after the Second World War, hoarding was natural behaviour. Farmers stockpiled rice against the possibility of crop failure or famine. When the oil crisis of 1973 struck, Japanese housewives panicked and stocked up on toilet tissue and detergent, causing severe shortages. This showed, he wrote, that 'our basic nature has not changed much'. And he concluded that modern industry has not changed much over the years either. But hoarding in industry is no longer practical, he said. 'Industrial society must develop the courage, or rather the common sense, to procure only what is needed, when it is needed and in the amount needed.' He said he developed the system from the idea of the modern supermarket. He says he originally heard about them from Kiichiro Toyoda, who had been to the United States years before, though he had never seen one. He got his chance on his first trip to the States in 1956 and was duly impressed. Although he visited General Motors and Ford automobile plants, it was the supermarkets that intrigued him, where customers only bought what they needed, when they needed it and in the amount they needed. The American supermarket managers filled the shelves with the amount of goods they expected to sell to fill the needs of the customers. Bingo. It was the just-in-time system, a rational system. It was while thinking about the supermarket structure that he got the idea of viewing the earlier process in the production line as a kind of store. The later process is the customer, who goes to the earlier process, the supermarket, to get the needed parts, the corn flakes or other foodstuffs.

Ohno worked for twenty years to get the production flow system working to his satisfaction, moving from one department of the manufacturing process to another. Through the years, as he finally became manager of the new Motomachi plant, he gained the confidence of the management, but 'getting people in every corner of the plant to understand naturally took a long time'. He said he could yell at a foreman under his own jurisdiction, but not at all those who probably could have benefited from it.

Ohno bragged that the true advantage of his system was its flexibility, its ability to keep a steady flow without high peaks and deep valleys. As an example, he cites the production of 10,000 Coronas in a month with twenty working days. The order is 5,000 sedans, 2,500 hardtops and 2,500 wagons. Instead of producing sedans until that part of the order is filled, and then hardtops and then wagons, the plant would build 250 sedans, 125 hardtops and 125 wagons a day, and run them this way: sedan, hardtop, sedan, wagon, sedan, and so forth. This way the production is level and the suppliers can also level their production.

Ohno liked to tell people that he was proud he was able to use old machinery and simple, common-sense techniques, despite the glittering promise of high technology. He was no Luddite but he liked to say, for example, that computers were essential in some aspects of the plant operation, particularly for scheduling, but the computer was a tool and he vowed not to be 'pushed around by it'. Likewise, he often referred to the fable of the tortoise and the hare, pointing out that high performance can be useless unless there is continuity, so that rushing to put out a lot of parts and then allowing the equipment to sit idle is another kind of waste. A machine's value is not measured by its years of service or its age, he said, but by the earning power it still has. He was never anxious to replace old machinery simply because it was depreciated or 'off the books'. His idea was to maintain equipment carefully and keep it as long as it earned its way. This is one reason Toyota, unlike Nissan, never made a display of massive numbers of expensive robots. And it is a lesson that General Motors learned to its cost when it saw robots as a solution to its problems and built a Detroit plant full of high-tech machines that never worked out.

There is a historical factor, seldom mentioned, that explains why one person, or a nation of people, might abhor waste, or *muda* in Japanese (Ohno also hated *mura*, or inconsistency, and *muri*, which means unreasonableness). Though today, seeing the disgusting piles of litter that are created after a night of revelry or a weekend when the cherry blossoms are out, or the rubbish on the climbing path up Mount Fuji, one would doubt Japan's aversion to waste. In public, the Japanese are wasters of packaging, chopsticks, cans, bottles and foodstuffs, at the same time sedulously separating their bottles, cans and paper for recycling at home. Industrially there is another story.

There is an expression once common in the United States that exists nowhere else that I know: 'There's plenty more where that came from.' The US is a nation blessed with just about everything – oil, coal, gas, helium, gold, silver, uranium, iron ore, bauxite, even diamonds. I was struck by this when Chevrolet ordered a recall of cars because of faulty axles. It seems a batch of axles which had been delivered to the assembly plant were inspected and many of them were found to be defective or out of specification. Naturally, the inspector, whose sole job it was to check the incoming parts, rejected the bad ones and tossed them into a separate bin. They could be scrapped, melted down or discarded. After all, there were plenty more where they came from. The only problem was that the container of bad axles somehow or other was delivered to the assembly line and the axles were installed on the Chevies. Nobody noticed that they were defective.

In Japan, there is not plenty more where anything came from. For older Japanese who remember the years of privation, the concept of waste carries deep connotations. Further, as a country that must import every ton of oil or iron ore, for example, wasting anything used to be described as a sin. The system of running large lots of goods and inspecting them later, without careful oversight of each piece, is a waste that Japanese industry has never got accustomed to. This is why Japanese companies are marvellous recyclers – Toyota even makes insulating material from the small percentage of scrapped car waste that can't be used for something else. The recyclability rate for Toyota cars is now about 85 per cent by weight and is expected to be 90 per cent by the year 2000.

TEACHING OTHERS

If it was difficult to explain the TPS to Japanese suppliers – and Ohno said it was – imagine the problem in dealing with foreigners. Toyota, with all of its assembly plants at one time almost in sight of each other, nevertheless had hundreds of suppliers feeding the hungry maw of the assembly lines. Trucks bearing parts were constantly moving to supply the products when needed. Although it all works without a sense of panic, there is a quiet sense of urgency. A team member riding a bicycle or a golf cart picks up the empty parts containers and strips the *kanban* cards from them, then delivers the cards to the room where they are collated and sorted by computer and dropped into boxes for the supplier company drivers to pick up, together with the collapsed containers.

Teruyuki Minoura, who is president of Toyota Motor Manufacturing North America (TMMNA), based in Cincinnati, was one of Ohno's minions as part of an élite squad called the Operations Management Consulting Division, designed to perfect TPS. 'At that time we were not doing much work. Basically we were lone wolves working on our own. Sometimes he would tell us about some company outside Toyota that was not making money, was in the red, so we were ordered to go out there and help them out. His instruction was, "Don't come back until that company is making money."

'We were at a loss, everybody. Then we figured out that his thought was that if you put somebody in a difficult position they will come up with something useful or valuable. Actually what we did at these supplier plants was to work at the plant level on a trial and error basis.' He and Cho decided that they needed some kind of theoretical underpinning for what they were doing, and they decided to write a book to bring all the elements together. The two of them came up with the name Toyota Production System.

The system was not everybody's favourite, even around Toyota City, the company town. There were complaints about the trucks racing through the streets to deliver parts to the factories. 'People began to criticize TPS in the national Diet (Japan's parliament), saying that Toyota was using the public road system as part of the company's conveyor belt.

'A newspaper reporter wanted to interview me about using the road system and I tried to explain it to him that we were levelling the usage of the road system over twenty-four hours. One of the basic concepts of TPS is the concept of *heijunka*, or levelling, so if you are talking of parts ordering, we order the same amount morning and evening with the same separation of time, frequency. The trucks will be running throughout the area all day at the same frequency. If you tried to transport all these things together at one time it would become overcrowded, and by levelling the production we were avoiding that.'

That made sense to the reporter, of course but, in actual fact, as Toyota's production grew, the road traffic became thicker and thicker. Toyota noted the increasing density of traffic and that added to motorist frustration was the possible danger to the environment and to safety in the crowded streets. When the newest Japanese assembly plant was built Toyota opted to locate it far away from Aichi, in Kyushu, Japan's southernmost main island. A major supplier and member of the Toyota Group, The Kanto Auto Works, which produces bodies for Toyota vehicles, also opened a new plant far away in Iwate prefecture and delivers its assemblies by boat instead of by truck.

An increasing number of parts and assemblies for Toyota vehicles are made by outside suppliers who operate within the TPS, supplying their products just-in-time. The industry is moving slowly toward production using a modular concept, where outside companies design, with the concurrence of the company, a fully completed component or set of components and deliver them directly to the assembly line. It is happening already. Chrysler in the US has been active in this area but the Japanese companies have not leapt in to embrace this method fully, though traditionally suppliers invest their talent and money to help to develop components for their client companies.

Hiromichi Kamimura is global customer director working with Toyota for Delphi Automotive Systems, a General Motors subsidiary which supplies a wide range of items – radiators, airbags, seats, wiring harnesses, brake systems, electronics and even audio systems – to the trade. In the Asia–Pacific region, for which Kamimura is vice-president, Toyota is the biggest customer. The company treats Delphi as a partner in its global operations. Kamimura calls the Japanese approach to modular production a 'prudent' one. 'They are ready to do it only if there are clear advantages in doing it.' Toyota, he adds, 'has excellent suppliers in Japan and the United States, so when we say we can offer them a modular product (it would mean) kicking out all others. They would say "don't be so greedy". In their view everybody must be happy. Toyota must see that it adds a certain value to the product. Actually, Toyota would tend to see it as a shift of jobs from Toyota sub-assembly to supplier assembly.'

The industry is definitely moving in that direction, particularly at European manufacturers, although they resisted for some time, says Kamimura. He insists that Delphi can do some things better than Toyota, 'and if modular construction results in a more rational product, with better functions and at lower costs', Toyota will accept more of it. Right now Delphi engineers work with Toyota engineers, planning ahead for components of the cars that are still on the drawing-board, attempting to come up with advanced new designs that Toyota can incorporate.

As lead times between models shorten from the old three to four years down to as little as two years it is critical that the companies supplying Toyota be insiders, attuned to the concepts and schedules of the company. Says Kamimura, 'We know they have to be changing their parts every model change. We know the Corolla keeps changing, for example, and they invite us to join in the development.'

Supplier companies have to jump through the Toyota hoop to do business; that is, they must embrace the system, and part of that is mutual benefit, including constant cost reduction. As TPS and growing Toyota business enables companies to become more profitable, Toyota has expected to share in those profits by means of reduced prices. Reducing inventories by just-in-time assembly is a considerable saving at Toyota, and it is designed to be a cost saving to the supplier who makes parts for Toyota just when needed and without a large inventory, and to the raw materials vendor who supplies the supplier. This was a concept easier to get across to Japanese companies, in which making a profit for hungry shareholders is not their reason for being, than to foreign firms, in which it is.

Delphi is a major supplier to New United Motor Manufacturing, Inc. (NUMMI) and to Toyota's other US manufacturing plants, as are a number of the company's 243 traditional parts and components suppliers. One issue that persistently came up in the battle with the US over Japanese imports into the States, and then over the activities of the new Japanese auto plants in the US, was their seeming reluctance to purchase parts from American companies that had long supplied the US industry. Some initial responses from the Japanese were that the reject rate of American parts was too high, but it was obvious to many that there was no eagerness to embrace foreign companies. For one thing, there was no basis for the kind of relationship the companies had with their suppliers at home. Logistics, logic and politics dictated that some suppliers had to be brought into the tent. But progress was slow.

HELP FOR SUPPLIERS

In 1992 then US President George W. Bush, on an official visit to Japan together with a group of automotive executives, in effect demanded that Japanese companies in Japan and at their North American units buy more parts from American suppliers. The ensuing talks did not go well. 'The American side kept saying Toyota is only interested in *selling* cars in the US,' says Hajime Ohba, who was the man to be entrusted with opening up TPS to US suppliers. 'They said, why don't we open the North American parts industry to them.' The Americans were exasperated, rueful that they had come at all, as so many of their minions had done in the 1980s, and warned that there would be some Congressional retaliation. Lesa Nichols, who is the manager of training and research at Toyota's US Supplier Support Center, set up in the wake of these talks, said, 'The Japanese were saying that the Americans can't really understand their perspective, and the US side was saying, "Well, help us understand it."' The project, from the American point of view, was a disaster. President Bush got sick at a formal government banquet and the meetings ended inconclusively. The Americans went away unhappy and the Japanese were relieved to see them go.

At Toyota there was continuing discussion on the topic of auto parts after the wreckage of the meeting was cleared away. Toyota was becoming a big player in the US market, and executives were concerned about their North American relationships, which included many points of contact with US parts makers in aid of their California and Kentucky ventures. It has about 400 American suppliers in 33 states. The Kentucky plant alone bought $3.7 billion worth of goods from American suppliers in 1997. But Toyota buys much less for its plants in Japan, where overseas shipment would be impossible for just-in-time manufacturing. Foreign investment in Japanese parts suppliers has not been successful, and few companies have the commitment of Delphi or several other giant international companies. Toyota decided to do something about the situation by setting up a Supplier Support Center in Lexington, Kentucky. Its mission: to teach interested companies TPS so they could prepare to sell to Toyota, or to anybody else who was interested. Says Ohba, who is vice-president of TMMNA and general manager of the center, 'Many top (Toyota) guys had discussions about what we could disclose to the (American) parts makers, and Shoichiro Toyoda decided it was TPS. He just decided we would do it. There was no discussion, it was just ordered.'

Ohba is a Toyota industrial engineer who has been working in Toyota's Operations Management Consulting Division since 1970, helping Toyota partners overseas improve their efficiency. When the decision was made to open up TPS to whatever North American companies were interested, Ohba was given the job. 'I was just called in and told to do it. I had no specific orders,' he says. Toyota also gave him a budget of $3.5 million and told him he could take one manager from Japan and hire twenty-one people in the States. Showing visitors through Toyota plants is a common courtesy that is generally reciprocal in the industry, and Toyota executives from the founder down to the current leadership acknowledge the openness and aid of foreign companies such as Ford, GM, Chrysler and Volkswagen. It did not seem an unnatural thing to do, considering the attention TPS was getting in the press.

In his first office in Lexington, Kentucky, Ohba had the help of Fujio Cho, who was president of the new Kentucky plant in nearby Georgetown, and he was on the phone a lot with Gary Convis, the executive vice-president of NUMMI, the GM-Toyota joint venture in California. 'I got my input from these people, and other managers. Mr Cho came to our office every morning and once a month we would visit a supplier and he would check to see if I was going in the right direction.'

When the announcements went out that Toyota was open to other companies interested in its production system, which by now had achieved widespread fame in the press and among managers and academics, there was a flurry of responses. Seventy-five companies inquired initially. There were many sceptics.

Ohba began a whirlwind series of meetings with executives at the interested companies. 'I had to see what kind of activity they had in place and I spent a lot of time on the shop floor not only with top management but also with floor people to gauge their willingness to change.' One thing was made explicit from the beginning, and that was that there would be no assumption that Toyota would take the company on as a supplier. There was no fee and no guarantee. It was a painstaking process. Companies that applied to learn the system included makers of automotive components such as exhaust systems, body panels, bumpers, air ducts, air bags, flywheels, seat recliner components, and general makers of glass, hospital beds, leather goods, office furniture and toys. Among them were famous names in American manufacturing such as A.O. Smith, TRW, Zenith and United Electric. To date, seventy-eight companies have participated in the program.

The TPS team has preconditions. The company has to agree there will be no reduction in workforce due to the implementation of the system. The last thing Toyota needs are a lot of laid-off workers blaming it for their plight. Besides, keeping people who are displaced by TPS improvements and using them elsewhere is part of the system. Companies have to pledge that top management will be consistently involved. They have to agree that their plant can function as a showcase to demonstrate the work of the Toyota Supplier Support Center (TSSC). And finally, as noted before, there should be no expectation of sales to Toyota because of their participation in the project.

The commitment to a company project is a four-phase process that requires seven months to a year. Most are completed in ten months. The entire project places clear-cut responsibilities on the management of the company, and enunciates just what the TSSC will do, wrapped up in a legal agreement. It requires classroom training and hands-on shop floor experience. In the beginning, simple demonstrations, such as one done at the TSSC office in Erlanger using large Lego blocks, show how production flow can and should work, and why conventional methods are inefficient.

Says Ohba, 'We usually start in the plant with one process, maybe shipping, assembly, welding, to demonstrate the total process. By using the existing facility with no investment we can get started using only cardboard or string to demonstrate the conversion from mass production to our process, so they get the basic idea.' Usually a company will use what is learned on one line to install the system on others. In fact the training is only the beginning, and companies soon realize that efficiencies depend on getting all their operations on the new lean system.

Nichols says one of the first things she hears from the participating companies once they have begun to understand the system is that mass production hides a lot of problems. 'When you take away the inventory,' she says, 'your security blanket is gone.

What we hear in the beginning when we put TPS in place is, "Hey, this is causing a lot of problems." But no, the problems were there before. Now they are going to be in your face and you are going to have to deal with them.' The system puts emphasis on repeatability, reliability, of doing every job in a specified period of time – they call it *takt* time, from the German word for rhythm.

In the first days of the project Ohba was on the road a lot, lining up the companies that were serious about learning the Toyota system. In one twenty-four-hour period he visited six plants in different cities. And within three years he accumulated one million frequent flyer miles on Delta Air Lines. He took one company president and the president of his plant's union local to Japan to see TPS in action because the company president knew he would need union cooperation and wasn't sure he could get it. Says Nichols, 'We should never talk in terms of a "union problem". We might have a people problem or a communications problem, which may mean we are not treating our people right. Our experience has been that both sides can work through their difficulties if they are really committed to frank discussions.'

THE HEART OF TPS

The much-vaunted TPS is the subject of erudite treatises, lengthy books and MBA case studies. But the system can be described in simple terms: just-in-time production can be implemented when a company distributes the work evenly, i.e. levels it. This involves getting up-to-date information from dealers on what kind of cars are being ordered and transmitting that to the factory, enabling it to have a daily production plan. Toyota boasts that it can supply a specific car to a customer in less than two weeks. The work is carefully designed to flow smoothly; workers are constantly productive, and neither the machinery nor the worker is ever idle. Workers are multi-skilled and machinery is designed to be flexible, so there is no build-up of parts, and workers are not waiting around for something to do while batches of parts are being made. During all this, workers are required to be involved in what they are doing, by inspecting parts as they use them, looking for defects. Further, on the final assembly line the area of a worker's responsibility is clearly marked. If he finds a defect, or he cannot finish his operation in the allotted time, he pulls the line-stop cord, which stops the line when it reaches the end of his position. A team leader or group leader will arrive to see what is wrong and come up with a solution. Often by the time the unit has reached the end of the team member's position he has worked out the problem and can cancel the line stop. The assembly lines at Toyota are equipped with many components that hark back to Sakichi's broken thread cut-off devices. If a sensor notes that an assembly is not in the proper position for the next operation, it will automatically stop the line and signal its position to the *andon*. This signalling process is called *jidoka*, from the Japanese word for automatic action. The entire system is built on what is called standardized work. Every job is thought out for maximum efficiency, and minimum effort or strain, though that is, of course relative in factory work. The other key element is *kaizen*, which means improvement or betterment, but which Toyota defines as 'constant improvement'. It is a crucial link in the relationship between the team member and the management. The team member is expected to be involved in his job and to seek ways of improving the quality of his work and the product he works on. He is not allowed to be a passive member watching the parts go by and adding his twist of the wrench; he is required to be an active participant. It is a tall order, and it explains why the job selection process at Toyota plants is such a complex and time-consuming one. Not everybody wants to give so much to a job.

Fujio Cho, in his introductory remarks for a lecture held in

Britain, said that sharing the concepts of TPS 'is one way of repaying the debt' that Toyota owes to Western traditions of manufacturing. He reminded his audience that before the Industrial Revolution, which began in England, a craftsman would make a whole product by himself, without a stockpile of semi-finished goods, and he converted raw materials into finished products quickly. 'In other words,' he said, 'he was a lean producer. His inventory was minimal. His production lead time for each bit of raw material was short. But he was not very productive, so he perished in the face of automation and specialization.

'What our predecessors did at Toyota was combine the lean efficiency of the craftsman with the gross productivity of mass production. They were the first people to recognize in-process inventories and long lead times as waste. This was an intuitive insight for Kiichiro Toyoda, the man who led Toyota into automobile manufacturing. Kiichiro had a gut feeling that manufacturing should proceed with a minimum of material on hand. He also had great ambitions for his automobile company. Kiichiro resolved in the early 1950s that Toyota should catch up with the Big Three US auto makers in productivity. That was a tall order for a company that was starting anew from nothing after a devastating war. But a production engineer by the name of Taiichi Ohno took the order seriously.' Cho told his audience about Ohno's hatred of waste in the accumulation of inventory, waste of movement and waste in overproduction and in overprocessing.

The Toyota Production System has proven workable in twenty nations outside of Japan, and indeed Lean Production, as it is now called generically, is being employed in companies far removed from automobiles and assembly lines. The MIT professors who awakened the world to Toyota's system with *The Machine That Changed the World* are now writing about *Lean Thinking*, and *Beyond Lean Thinking*.

'We continue to find new ways to accommodate people of

different nationalities and cultures,' said Cho. 'And we find ways to streamline the flow of work in sectors besides manufacturing.' He said Toyota is now trying to improve after-sales service by handling replacement parts on a just–in–time basis, and just–in–time improvements are reducing dealer inventories. 'Lean manufacturing at Toyota,' he declared, 'is a living and ever-changing concept.'

At Japanese plants abroad, the cafeterias always have some Japanese food items on the menu. It is a comfort to the Japanese and a reminder and encouragement to the foreign workers of the internationalization of the effort. One day a team member at the Kentucky plant presented Cho with his improvement on the ancient oriental dining device, chopsticks, with which foreigners have struggled for years. The inventive team member had mounted his chopsticks on a clothespin that could be conveniently flexed like forceps.

'This,' says a chuckling Cho, 'is also *kaizen*.'

CHAPTER FIVE
SELLING TO THE WORLD

Optimism and self-satisfaction were running high on a hot day in August 1957, when the first Toyota cars reached the United States. European importers had identified the neglected small car niche in the US market, and Volkswagen's Beetle and Renault's Dauphine were fighting for market share with a few lesser models. VW would be the winner, but surely, they thought in Toyota City, there was room for one more in the giant American market of ten million cars a year. It is a bit of automotive folklore that a lowly American consul in Japan gave Toyota Motor Sales President Taizo Ishida the encouragement he needed to export the new Crown to the US. In fact the company decided to try the US market after Shotaro Kamiya, the president of Toyota Motor Sales (TMS), noted the small car phenomenon on a trip to the US in 1955, as did Ishida when he visited bank officials in Washington, DC a year later. The decision to try it was made quickly, and without any valid research of the market.

On this brilliant southern California day two gleaming Crowns were gingerly lowered on to the dock, the deluxe model dolled up with big white-sidewall tyres. They were greeted with polite applause by Seisi Kato and his assistants and a few curious onlookers. A knot of newsmen and photographers was on hand to watch the local Miss Japan bestow a bouquet of flowers on the cars as a sign of welcome.

Seisi Kato of TMS was in charge of the operation and he remembers that the idea of selling Japanese passenger cars in the United States, 'seemed then like some wild dream'. Of that first day he later wrote that he was 'brimming over, if it's possible, with both enthusiasm and anxiety as I watched the first of our cars depart from the docks'. In the next few days the reaction of prospective dealers was encouraging, although Big Three dealers shunned the little upstart. People who had seen the pictures in the local papers called to ask where they could buy one. Though rather clunky and stolid looking now, for its day the car was marginally stylish. It was boxy and heavy, and it had borrowed sheet metal lines from Chevrolet and others. The car boasted such amenities as two-speed windshield wipers, a light that warned of a door ajar, and a locking gas cap. Six people could squeeze into it, and it would, theoretically, deliver 33 miles a gallon from its seemingly husky little engine. On the slim evidence of the initial reaction, it seemed to Kato and his colleagues that there was great market potential in California and the US as a whole, and in the flush of nervous enthusiasm they reckoned that they could sell 400–500 a month, or easily 10,000 units a year. At the time that would be a huge order, and Toyota Motor would have to raise its production levels to accommodate it.

All systems seemed go – until they collapsed. Although the car was popular and seemed peppy in the low-speed and narrow roads of Japan, at 80 miles an hour on the Los Angeles freeways it turned out to be a dud. At sustained high speed the engine vibrated alarmingly and power dropped. On the hot, high Mojave desert road between Los Angeles and Las Vegas, a well-travelled route, the engine overheated. The car was, as it turned out, built like a tank, overpriced and underpowered. 'Our dreams', said Kato later, 'sank like a ship with a hole in the bottom.' He wanted to give up, but back in Japan cool heads insisted that the company stay registered, keep open the salesroom in Hollywood, and try to sell as many cars as possible just to keep in the game until decisions could be made as to what to do next. Fixes could be made on upcoming versions of the car. For another thing there was the four-wheel-drive Toyota Land Cruiser, which was developed on a truck platform during the Korean War for the US military, and was a proven workhorse. It had been selling well in Latin America since the early 1950s; surely it could be sold in the US.

By the end of 1958 the US sales office had sold a grand total of 287 cars and one Land Cruiser. But soon the Land Cruiser became the mainstay of Toyota sales until the factory could come back from the drawing-board with an acceptable passenger car. An improved model of the Crown, the Tiara, was sent to the States, but it was not a hit. Finally, in 1960 it was decided to stop passenger car exports until the company could build a car suitable for US, and later Australian, highways and long-distance travel. Toyota's rival, Nissan, then attempting to sell the early Datsuns cars in America, had similar difficulty in coping with this radically different market. In fact former Datsun salesmen recall being secretly delighted when one shipment of cars arrived at the Port of Houston badly damaged. They could collect the insurance and didn't have to try to sell them to a resistant public.

At home Toyota developed sales systems that were suited to the market, and fulfilled the hopes of Toyota's bankers when they insisted on splitting the sales from the manufacturing functions. The company always seemed to find the kind of people who could apply reasoned and sometimes unorthodox techniques to move the product. They were not in the stereotypical image of the Japanese salaryman. As a new company before the Second World War Toyota was nothing if not inventive. Searching around for sales talent they found their man at General Motors of Japan.

THE GOD OF SALES

His name was Shotaro Kamiya, a thoughtful, soft-spoken, self-made man when he was invited to join Toyota as sales manager in 1935. Although only in his thirties, he had already had a successful sales career representing the giant Mitsui trading company in Seattle and then London. He was cosmopolitan and shrewd, a match for the automotive men then in Japan for foreign companies and for the Toyota rivals in Tokyo. 'I was ambitious,' he told me several years before his death in 1980. 'I didn't want to work for Mitsui for ever, so while I was in England I set up my own export house, selling steel to Japan.' The Great Depression dried up the market and he returned to Japan. But because of his contacts in Britain and the US he was offered sales positions in distributorships in Japan by both Ford and General Motors. Ford offered him a high salary, he said, but GM offered him only commission. A hotshot salesman, he took the commission job because he knew he could make more money that way than with Ford's salary. The prelude to war stifled his career as the American car makers were shoved out and the military leaders demanded production of trucks for its depredations on the continent of Asia. At Toyota after the end of the war 'we were in debt, nobody had any money. We couldn't pay wages and we had labour trouble. I decided something had to be done.' As he tells it, 'I left the main company and set up a specialized sales company. The main principle was that my company would buy the cars from the production company and the production company could then pay its wages and wouldn't have to worry (about mine).' He was confident that he could sell cars. 'By separating,' he said, 'each unit could concentrate on its own problems. We concentrated on sales, promotion, export, financing. We had to build special piers, ships to carry cars for export, but the production company didn't have to pay a yen for them.'

Most importantly, he said, 'We can work very closely on what kind of cars we should make, give advice to Toyota Motor.' The other advantage to the Toyota Motor Company was that, as the bankers hoped, it would only produce cars that were ordered by TMS. He kept the stocks lean, purposely. Under his direction dealer stocks amounted to only about 70 per cent of one month's sales, thereby keeping inventories low.

Kamiya's strategy for selling in the US was to start out on the West Coast, to build up dealership and service, and then, once proven and with a good reputation for service, move toward the east. He was embarrassed by the failed first attempt. 'The Crown just wasn't made well enough to compete,' he said. 'Too heavy, too slow, uneconomical, poorly made.' Kamiya's idea was that it would not be wise to try to compete with the type of cars the American makers sold. He thought 'if you don't eat into their market there should be no trouble'. He felt that American companies might build smaller cars, and perhaps come down to the 2,000 cc engine size but not lower. 'This is why I decided to push the small, 1,900 cc Corona. We gave it a good finish, and some extras, at low cost.' As a Crown replacement, the Corona became a hit in the US, the start of a long success story.

For many years Kamiya was tremendously powerful within the Toyota organization, influencing the styling, the materials and the production schedules. He created Toyota's dealership network in Japan, bringing in some former General Motors dealers. Kamiya also persuaded the affable and talented Seisi Kato to leave GM and join the new company right after he made the jump himself, so he would have the basis of a good staff.

Early on Kamiya had been stirred by Kiichiro Toyoda's patriotic vow to build Japanese automobiles with Japanese hands and was trying to put together a team with the Toyoda family to fulfil the dream. He needed experienced, talented people, and few were available. Kato would be a catch, but he was hesitant. When Kato visited the Toyota plant he was shocked by how primitive it was, compared with the GM assembly operation. Kamiya was, in Kato's words, relentless. He finally sent Kato a telegram reading: 'Have some conviction. Join me!' When Kato quit GM in 1935 his fellow workers laughed at him. If they only knew! His starting salary was half his GM salary, and when he arrived at Toyota to take up his job the introduction of the first model was three weeks away 'and not a single vehicle had been assembled, and no sales preparations had been made at all'. Kato was to be Kamiya's right-hand man for nearly fifty years, and succeeded him as president, when Kamiya moved up to the ceremonial post of chairman.

After the war Toyota salesmen were soon ubiquitous in Tokyo's cities and villages. They not only sold cars, they conducted market research, and what amounted to social research, on their rounds, selling cars door to door. Unlike the Western system in which glittering showrooms entice people to visit and test-drive cars and then negotiate a deal, the custom in Japan is still intensely personal. Toyota and other makers have showrooms, and are now trying to encourage more and more people to visit them and make their car buying decisions there. But the door to door visit of salesmen is still the backbone of the system. Even today, some young Toyota recruits are expected to make 'cold' personal calls on prospective clients to get a feel for the business and impress them with the importance of being close to the market and the customers. Toyota salesmen gather detailed data on families through the generations, their history of car buying, the lives of their children, and some grow to be very close to the families they serve, helping them select a car. They often take care of licensing, financing and insurance for them. When there is car trouble, or the biennial inspection is due, the buyers frequently call the salesman, who arranges to help them. Greeting cards and small gifts on important family occasions, at year end or midyear holidays, are often expected from the salesmen. Customers thus tend to remain brand loyal, and the company gets an updated data bank on customer preferences, complaints, likes and dislikes that helps to determine what kind of products it will eventually produce. The other side of the coin is that occasionally an eager salesman will get into financial trouble by offering a client a deal he has to finance partially by himself from proceeds of other sales past or yet to come. (The financial periodical *Barron's* wrote of some cases of salesmen pushed to financial extremes by franchise dealers demanding sales.)

Kamiya was also influential in setting up the sales channels through which the cars are handled in the domestic market. Instead of brand name divisions, such as GM's Chevrolet, Buick, Pontiac, Oldsmobile and Cadillac divisions, Toyota's sales outlets handle specific models of Toyota cars and other vehicles.

By 1965 Toyota had created a new passenger car, the Corona, which was powerful, sturdily built, acceptably styled, had an automatic transmission and an optional air conditioner, and was priced just under $2,000. It was an instant success. It took only ten years to overtake Volkswagen as the number one import in the US. In Japan it was advertised leaping through the air, crashing through barriers and rolling over, yet ready to run after such rough treatment. The campaign, overseen by Kato, boosted sales markedly, and pleased Kamiya.

Kamiya was so influential and so well known in Japan that he was openly referred to in the press as 'The God of Sales' for Toyota. He was a modest man and didn't like the title, although it is worth noting that in Japan the acknowledged leader in any field is often referred to as a god. Thus the most famous comic book artist is called the god of comics. The title is respectful but doesn't actually refer to things ecclesiastical.

However, when Kato gave a press conference after taking over from Kamiya he said he preferred to remain mortal, and one magazine headlined its story: 'Presidency of Toyota Motor Sales Shifts from God to Man'.

TRIAL AND ERROR ABROAD

TMS representatives sent abroad had no blueprints to follow. They had to make up their methods as they went along. And they sometimes brought with them original ideas that would make a Westerner blanch. They were, and some are today, an original breed, quite unlike the sophisticates of the giant, ponderous and self-aggrandizing firms of Tokyo. The perversely proud 'bumpkins' from Aichi prefecture were unashamed of their unpretentiousness. They were willing to try anything that worked. And the home office held its breath, sometimes its tongue. The enterprise could be unorthodox.

When Yukiyasu ('Call me Yuki') Togo was sent to Thailand in 1970 he stepped into a hotbed of anti-Japanese sentiment. Japanese offices were being vandalized and Japanese factories plagued by strikes.

'I was sent there to be marketing manager,' says Togo, 'and I realized that there was no way I could get to the people and sell cars if I didn't have the language. There was no communication. It was one of the things they were mad about, that the Japanese businessmen were not making a sincere effort to understand and work in Thai society. They were trying to do everything Japanese style in a non-Japanese culture.'

Togo began studying the language before work every morning and before long he could hold a simple conversation in Thai. But it wasn't enough. 'I soon realized how vital the Buddhist religion is to the Thais,' he says. It is a different branch of Buddhism from the *Zen* he studied at the Enkakuji Temple in Kamakura just after the war. Besides, in Kamakura he hadn't learned a lot. He was always fighting with the other acolytes and his master kicked him out, saying he was not suited to lead a life of asceticism. 'I was a wild boy,' he admits. He didn't outgrow it. In fact, just after Seisi Kato hired him, he says, 'I immediately formed the "Corps of Independent-Minded Hoodlums" and did just about whatever I pleased. I was brazen.' He was a daredevil race car driver, a private pilot who would in pre-retirement fly his Cessna around the world, a golfer, a water skier and a free thinker. He also sang 'My Way' on the stage in Las Vegas with Wayne Newton.

In Bangkok he got to know members of the Royal Family and at a tea party he mentioned to the King Mother that he was interested in Buddhism. The next day an emissary from the Ministry of Religion appeared at Toyota Thailand's offices and told Togo's boss, the president of Toyota Thailand, that the Ministry would assist Togo in his desire to learn more about Thai Buddhism. It was an invitation Togo's boss would not allow him to refuse. Togo shaved his head and eyebrows and was admitted to the Marble Temple of the Royal Palace, where he became a monk. As he recalls it, 'This was an incredible and humbling experience. Every morning after sleeping on a hard mat I woke up very early, took my alms bowl and went begging barefooted in the streets for my only meal of the day.' Togo says he learned a lot about Thailand from that experience. When he returned to his company after a few weeks he had the respect of his Thai employees. Toyota's operation suffered no labour disruptions after that and he feels his short stint as a monk helped.

But Toyota Motor Sales was no particular respecter of sales managers turned monks. It was having trouble selling cars in Canada, where it was assembling them from kits shipped in from Japan, and so Togo was named president of Toyota Canada. His mission was to improve sales. He spoke only poor English but that didn't intimidate him. To energize his staff he announced that he was going to try door to door selling. 'They thought this was a crazy idea.' The method in his madness was that he would learn something about ordinary Canadian people this way, about the way they live, and perhaps find out just what the marketing problems were first hand.

'I wanted to catch the family members at home together, so every evening after work I went out into the neighbourhood and called on several families. Some treated me nicely and welcomed me into their homes. Others slammed the door in my face, but I learned and Toyota learned.' Togo visited more than one hundred Canadian homes, and he also sold seven cars. Like many others at Toyota, Togo, though he is retired, will still try to sell you a Toyota. 'One time I sold a car to a *yakuza*, a gangster,' he recalls, 'and he said he wouldn't pay unless I cut off my finger. Sometimes it gets a little too colourful.'

To get Toyota more entrenched in Canada he conceived the idea of utilizing one of Canada's prime commodities to address the balance of trade issue. He proposed to Toyota City that Toyota begin manufacturing wheels of Canadian aluminium in western Canada for shipment to Japan. Eiji Toyoda liked the idea and he sent Takeshi Nagaya, who is now president of Toyota Motor Corporate Services of North America (TMCS), to Canada to start up the project. It was particularly successful, says Nagaya, because the yen was cheap when he bought the manufacturing equipment from Japan, and by the time the plant went into operation the yen appreciated 'and we were in a position to sell products to Toyota, Japan, at a very good price. Before I went back to Japan we decided to double the capacity.'

Togo stayed in Canada for eight years, gaining a reputation for his breezy, friendly attitude and for handing out round calling cards with his picture on them. By the time he was assigned to head Toyota Motor Sales USA (TMSUSA), based in southern California, he had already learned a lot about the American market, and about working with dealers. 'Go for it. That's my theme,' he liked to tell his staff. 'Sell like hell.'

When he arrived in California something about the Toyota image was bothering him. 'At that time,' he says, 'Toyota's name had a kind of low-cost image. A good car but inexpensive. Unfortunately, the yen/dollar situation caused us to increase our price, so I had to launch some kind of campaign saying that our cars are expensive but well worth it.'

LEXUS: UP TO THE FIRST FLOOR

'But maybe what we need is a luxurious car that would create a new image, a car of high quality, perhaps even up-market of the Mercedes-Benz. That is what I aimed for.' The thought of it makes his eyes light up. 'I argued strongly and pushed and tried to sell my idea to my boss and the executives, but most of the executives were not in favour. They said my plan would not be successful. But I am a salesman and always, when I hear a negative comment, I feel I must challenge it.'

That wasn't all. He thought an expensive car should be sold in a separate sales channel. As he puts it, 'If you go to a department store in Japan you find low-cost goods being sold in the basement, but on the first floor you have higher-priced goods. You cannot sell a fur coat in the basement of a department store. I had to convince people and overcome their resistance, but I was lucky enough to be able to do it.' He was aiming at the Mercedes market.

As luck would have it, Toyota had a possible car design being prepared for the commemoration of the company's fiftieth anniversary, says Togo. It was already in the form of a clay model and it looked good. He soon was able to drive the prototype on Toyota's test track in Hokkaido with his wife at his side, 'wearing a helmet and going 150 miles an hour', and he liked it. He then asked the design team to come to the US and stay for three or four months 'to get the feeling of rich people'. He arranged for them to meet many of his friends, including politicians, businessmen and golf pros, to understand something of their lifestyle and the kind of quality they were accustomed to. The dealers who sold the cars, the salespersons and others who would come in contact with Lexus buyers, Togo speculated, should also be people sensitive to quality and a luxurious lifestyle. It would be a tough bill to fit.

Lexus was an expensive gamble, even though Honda success-fully introduced their version of an up-market car in 1986, and Nissan was on their way to producing their version, Infiniti, later. Togo was putting together an upscale network of dealers. Aided by his vice-president, Bob McCurry, a Chrysler veteran known for his uncompromising demands on dealers (at Chrysler they nicknamed him 'Captain Crunch'), Togo picked a cadre of successful and well-financed dealers to set up separate, high-quality facilities to sell and service the new car.

A week before the car was to be announced at the Detroit Auto Show, in January, 1989, Lexus was given an unexpected and unwelcome setback. The car was in production; its advertis-ing was set, signage was being installed, the name was emblazoned on the engines and escutcheons attached to bonnets and boot lids. Then a judge ruled that the Lexus name couldn't be used. The Mead Corporation, which owned the legal computer data-base called Lexis claimed infringement and a federal judge heard the case. Toyota brought linguists into court to testify that one could pronounce the two names distinctly, though, embarrass-ingly, they often had to spell out which one they meant. Togo's audacious decision to go ahead with the launch anyway paid off. On appeal the way was cleared for the use of the name, the ruling being that the nature of the businesses were so dissimilar that it was unlikely that the two would be confused. The publicity managed to give Lexus a big boost in the name recognition it needed as a newcomer. Its commercials were also memorable. A favourite was of a Lexus on a dynamometer, its engine effortlessly spinning its wheels at 60 miles an hour while a pyramid of champagne glasses perched on the bonnet, quite still.

The launch was auspicious. The selling price was well below that of the target Mercedes, and automotive journalists mar-velled at the quality. One Detroit automotive editor remembers test-driving the car from his home to his office: 'Here I am driving this car to work and it is absolutely perfect. I thought, what am I going to write about? There's nothing wrong with it.'

Well, not exactly. Soon there were complaints that Lexus was a bit stodgy looking, and then only weeks after the car was put on the market a defect was noted in the rear brakes. Toyota engineers said the problem was insignificant, and could be fixed during routine maintenance. Togo insisted the cars be recalled. A formal recall would draw attention to the defect and it would be widely reported in the press, so Togo's sales colleagues argued that the engineers were not concerned and neither should they be. A recall would only invite adverse publicity that would hurt sales. 'I argued with them,' Togo says, but the decision was his to make. 'I said, this is a way to create credibility, so let's start the recall.' It was an expensive thing to do: owners were notified that, if they wished, their car would be picked up and fixed overnight. The cars were returned the next day freshly washed and full of fuel. Togo was prepared for criticism. 'Actually, I wrote out my resignation letter and submitted it to my boss in case it wasn't successful, so I could take full responsibility,' says Togo. Fortunately it was very successful. The press was all over the story, putting the recall in a favourable light, quoting owners who marvelled at the efficiency of the operation. They liked the little touches, such as the full tank of petrol. Such a recall had not been seen in the US before.

Togo also became a fixture on the charitable scene in the United States and particularly in southern California. Togo's successor Yoshio Ishizaka last year received the Whitney Young Award of the Los Angeles Urban League for Toyota's efforts in building an automotive training centre in troubled south central Los Angeles. So far nearly five hundred minority people have graduated from the course, and 80 per cent of them have been placed in jobs.

Although Togo is retired and living in Hawaii, he is still an honorary adviser to Toyota Motor Sales USA and can sometimes be found at headquarters, when he isn't on the golf-course. The other day he was playing golf with his wife at Rolling Hills and, says Togo, 'I met a friend, so I called my dealer and said I want to introduce my friend Mr Kasuga, who wants to trade in his Mercedes. I sold him a GS-400.'

ROILING MAGMA

Toshiaki (Tag) Taguchi, who is North and Latin American sales Managing Director based in Tokyo, remembers those wild early days. 'All we knew about the United States then was what we had seen in the movies. I was surprised by the freeways, and all the cars. We had a network of small dealers including Hollywood Toyota, owned by Toyota, and we hoped we could finally sell some cars.' It was the mid-1960s, and Taguchi was soon assigned to the east coast, where cars were being imported at Newark for the sparse network of dealers in the eighteen eastern states. 'We had no fax in those days. Communication was by telex paper tape, and airmail. I don't recall ever calling Japan on the phone.'

In 1997, Toyota sold 1.3 million cars in the US, 60 per cent of them built in North America. 'It's quite a significant change we have experienced,' says Taguchi proudly. Yet Toyota dealers now complain they can't get enough cars to sell. In fact the gauntlet was thrown down at the 1998 dealers' meeting in Las Vegas by Yoshio Ishizaka, Togo's successor as president and CEO of TMSUSA. He challenged the dealers to sell two million Toyota and Lexus vehicles in the year 2000. 'I know what you are thinking,' said Ishizaka, holding out a figuratively restraining hand. 'How can we do it when we can barely supply you with enough vehicles now? Over the next few years two-thirds of the vehicles will roll off the line right here (in North America), and you will have the production.' Hiroshi Okuda, TMC president, outlined the increases in production the US and Canadian plants will make – including boosting Canada to 200,000 Corollas and Camry Solaras, Georgetown, Kentucky to 500,000 Camrys, Siennas and Avalons, and from the new Indiana plant 150,000 units of new vehicles, Tundra pickups and a new Sport Utility Vehicle (SUV). The total output of all Toyota plants in the US and Canada will reach more than one million, making Toyota the first international company to hit the one million unit production level in North America. He also promised them a new entry level vehicle, referred to only as the NBC, a new basic car, positioned against the Ford Escort and the Nissan Sentra, two new sports cars for young buyers, and the ingenious, economical and environmentally clean hybrid Prius for the year 2000. And there would be more.

Gaining market share and making a profit in the US market is not easy, Taguchi agrees. 'You have over 200 million people and more than 100 million vehicles,' he says, 'but the market itself is constantly changing, like an active volcano – the mountain is the same but inside the magma is roiling.

'Today, more than 50 per cent of the market is SUVs, pickup trucks and minivans. When I first went to the US those vehicles were mainly for commercial use; ordinary people almost never drove them, except for small pickup trucks. The American market may be 15 million to 17 million new vehicles a year, but the type of vehicle people want will reflect the dynamism of the industry.'

He points to the SUV as 'one sign of the mature market, which means that the people want to have something different. We have had the Land Cruiser around for forty years but we never thought we could sell them in big volume. But when we introduced the 4-Runner we were actually one of the pioneering groups in developing the compact SUVs and minivans, even before Chrysler introduced their very popular minivan. You have to keep your eyes on the market. One day you may have a certain market share but if you don't work hard enough relative to the competitors, two or three years later – the cycle of model changes is shorter now – it will be a completely different picture.'

Although Toyota boasts about its internet site as a marketing tool and is encouraging dealers to improve their own sites as an aid to selling, Taguchi is sceptical of the notion that large numbers of people will buy cars over the internet. 'You have to have a point of outlet,' he argues 'where people can test-drive and make a deal. Even in Japan more people are test-driving today; it is a social trend.' He concedes that in Japan people have grown accustomed to buying a car out of a catalogue, or having a single model brought around to the house to try out, but he says that is changing. In the US it is possible to tell an internet dealer intermediary how much you want to pay for a specific car and the intermediary tries to find the car at your price. Europe has several major discounters who do virtually the same. The industry is not comfortable with this. 'In today's society,' says Taguchi, 'customers have to understand the need (for dealers) to have a certain reasonable profit. I am hopeful that, even when the internet develops, common sense will prevail.'

The public's dissatisfaction with the old fashioned horse-trading method of making 'deals' is driving the search for other, less stressful and more straightforward ways of buying the family transportation. The entire industry is aware that the buying experience is considered distasteful by many people. 'This is our challenge,' says Taguchi. He notes that J.D. Power and Associates, which does detailed surveys of customer satisfaction – Toyota was one of Power's first clients – has found that, while the Lexus division is always in the top three in sales satisfaction, the Toyota division 'is at the bottom end of the ranking but we are trying to improve'.

Ishizaka, who came to TMS USA as president and CEO in 1996, has spent his almost four decades with Toyota in its overseas operations, from Europe to the Middle East, the Far East, Oceania and finally the US. His three sons are multilingual. Ishizaka says the customers deserve good treatment; after all, it is their money.

'I don't like the term "deal". We have to set quality and true value as standards. Today it is possible to find out dealer cost on the internet and the dealers and manufacturers have to learn to cope with this.'

The old Japanese door to door method is inefficient, he agrees, and it would probably not be feasible to try to start it elsewhere. In Japan Toyota is holding special sales events to bring customers into its new showrooms. And there is more emphasis on selling used cars. But the salespeople still like to follow up with the customers. 'It is more of a courtesy,' says Ishizaka. 'The customer feels like he's king if the salesman comes to his home. Even though the system is beginning to change, customers often ask salesmen to come home afterwards,' and salespeople are usually eager to do so. One reason the Japanese salesmen like to visit the home of a buyer is that the credit reporting system in Japan is still primitive and a visual check of the home might alert the salesman to a poor credit risk.

If Toyota is going to sell 1.5 million vehicles a year in the US, Ishizaka says the sales organization will have to grow, develop and change, the three pillars of Ishizaka's edifice. 'I want that to be profitable growth,' he insists. But analysts have in the past, and continue, to question Toyota's profitability. Certainly vehicles such as the RAV4 EV, which is leased to utility companies, and the coming hybrid Prius, which, industry analysts say, sells at a loss in Japan right now, will be a drag on profits, though this may be balanced by new models such as the truck and the SUVs, which are in themselves hugely profitable. The Prius, it is argued, is likely to attract customers to Toyota showrooms, even if sales of the car are slow.

Yale Gieszl, as executive vice-president of the TMS, USA, spends a lot of his time talking to US dealers. He joined Toyota after working on the account for Price Waterhouse. He found the company so different from any firm he had worked with as an accountant – for one thing they actually welcomed him to the office – that he didn't have any hesitation when they asked him to join. 'They sent me a basket of fruit at my office in downtown LA during the holidays back in 1968 or 1969,' he recalls. 'Nobody sends their auditor a basket of fruit at Christmas. I was the envy of the office. Auditors are so disliked by companies they audit. But not this one.'

Yuki Togo used to pass out $50 cheques when some company milestone was reached. In 1998 everybody at headquarters, no matter what the job classification, got $50 from Ishizaka in recognition of a sales milestone. Says Gieszl: 'We just wanted to say thank you and say everybody is important and contributed to this milestone. It wasn't a lot of money but it was enough to take your spouse out to dinner.'

Perhaps the flamboyant days are gone, but the company is still human.

CHAPTER SIX
TOE IN THE WATER

As the 1980s unfolded two other Japanese auto makers – Honda and Nissan – took the plunge and set up plants in the United States, but Toyota hesitated, teetering at the water's edge. I asked Shoichiro Toyoda then why Toyota was waiting. Without a smile, he said that, despite what success other ventures might eventually claim, he questioned if it would be possible to make a profit in such a venture in the high-cost environment of the US. The others had their reasons for moving production offshore. Honda had run out of plant capacity in Japan and moved into Marysville, Ohio to build two-wheelers at first, before going into production of cars, and whether they were actually making a profit wasn't clear. Besides, Honda's quota under the restraint system was small. Nissan's move into Tennessee appeared quite successful, but its profitability was also in question. Both have had persistent labour trouble. Overriding it all was the fluctuating yen/dollar relationship, which for a time was to make the US a lower-cost venue than Japan.

As Toyoda recalls it today, 'We did not have the confidence to set up a plant [in the US] on our own, so we studied the possibility of having a tie-up with someone, perhaps a joint venture. Historically we had had many opportunities from prior to the war, when we had made attempts to merge with Ford.' True, the first attempt was made as early as 1939, when a three-way arrangement that included Nissan was discussed with Ford but died a natural death as the Second World War loomed. A technical agreement was talked about in 1950 and another arrangement was sought in 1960. None of them bore fruit.

The more recent talks with Ford began with high hopes,

partially because of the long, if arm's-length, relations between the two companies in the past. Eiji Toyoda proposed the talks in a letter in 1980 to Donald Peterson, who was then president of Ford. The proposal was to assemble a car designed by Toyota for distribution by Ford and Toyota dealers in the US. The assembly would take place at a Ford plant that was no longer in operation.

It seemed like a logical and workable plan, but the devil was in the details. Although some Ford executives were cool to the idea in general, the sticking point was the crucial question: what kind of car to produce? Ford rejected Toyota's proposal for a compact car it had in the works (the Camry, eventually to become one of the best-selling cars in the US) because Ford had somewhat similar models (the Topaz and the Tempo) due to be introduced a couple of years later. Other models were discussed and finally the sides agreed to test Toyota's Hi-Ace minivan. The automotive and business press were excited about the possible deal, and estimates of the number of as-yet-unknown vehicles this as-yet-unnamed plant would produce ran as high as 600,000 a year. Neither side had any such grandiose plans. Rather they were thinking of starting at about 200,000. Toyota designers reworked the Hi-Ace and sent a full-size model of the vehicle, fashioned in plastic, to Ford. A focus group was assembled to examine and critique it. Then, disaster. Their comments were unflattering enough to rule out the Hi-Ace, which left both sides where they had started. Prof. Stephen E. Weiss, in a 1997 paper on such negotiations between companies, wrote that the report of the Ford focus group left Toyota executives 'shocked'. The rejection from Ford was the 'first and final blow'.

'Well,' says Toyoda today, 'we could not stand by and do nothing. We commissioned two or three firms, including SRI and Nomura, to actually look into the potential of Toyota setting up factories in the US. Eventually, we had conversations with General Motors.' These came about after contacts beginning in

1982 between GM Chairman Roger Smith and Seisi Kato, chairman of Toyota Motor Sales, who had worked for GM in Japan before he joined Toyota in 1935. Smith proposed talks that might lead to a 50/50 joint venture. GM had studied ways to improve productivity and quality through the use of robots and quality circles but had not been successful. A joint venture would give them a chance to analyse the Toyota system in depth. For Toyota, such a plan would give them instant entry into the US labour market, where it could learn first hand whether American labour could produce Toyota-quality cars. It could also learn more about the problems their competitors faced in the US.

'The first person I contacted at GM was Jack Smith, who is now chairman, but he was then in global product planning,' says Shoichiro Toyoda. 'We discussed what kind of automobile would be good, and we decided that it should be made at a factory that was then closed. Ultimately we decided to use the Fremont plant. We encouraged Roger Smith to meet with Eiji Toyoda, who was then president of the Toyota Motor Co. Although we hadn't completed plans yet, we felt that when the information leaked out we needed to have the discussions under way.' The car was a version of Toyota's sub-compact Sprinter, in the Corolla class, and it would be marketed as a Chevrolet Nova.

'As to the plant, although there were several locations available, we thought the west coast would be preferable because it was close to Japan and because of the good port facilities in Oakland and the transportation infrastructure. One of our concerns was the possibility of earthquakes until we were assured that the Fremont site had always been very stable.' He pauses for a second, 'we also had a survey company look into the area and we heard very negative comments about the attitude of the employees. However, overall, we felt this was the place.'

There were hurdles to be overcome before anybody was going to build cars at Fremont. One was that the new company itself,

New United Motor Manufacturing, Inc., (NUMMI) a joint venture. Ford, Chrysler and American Motors immediately opposed the new deal as a violation of US antitrust laws. Then there was labour. GM had contracts with the United Auto Workers union at its plants all across North America. There was no way Fremont could be reactivated without some accommodation with the UAW. The legal challenges from the other auto makers were surmounted, and the Federal Trade Commission approved the project in April 1984, with Tatsuro Toyoda, brother of Shoichiro, as president.

The labour agreement the negotiators hammered out with the UAW was a landmark in American labour history. At Fremont, two hundred or more unskilled job classifications were integrated into one, and skilled jobs into three. The skilled trades classifications were likewise shrunk. The old system of having workers doing one single operation at a specific pay scale was to be scrapped. At NUMMI all workers would become multi-skilled through intensive training, for part of which some would go to Japan. (An experienced labour negotiator says that when Toyota officials lamented the labour situation, GM told Toyota that they would simply not even try to go non-union, and Toyota went along.)

To fashion a labour agreement they called in former Secretary of Labor William Usery, a skilled labour negotiator. Says one of the principals, 'He had to convince the UAW they had the greatest thing to gain, which is jobs.'

Shoichiro Toyoda says everybody at Toyota was relieved and delighted when the new agreement, the first of its kind, was signed. 'A trust was established between the American workers and Japanese management,' he says. Since then the negative attitude many Japanese executives used to have about the quality of American labour was proved wrong. As to the labour troubles at the old Fremont plant under GM, 'I don't believe the American workers were at fault. What is important is that there be trust between management and the workers. I have seen a considerable number of other plants in the United States and I've noticed that if the individual heading the plant is a fine person the company itself does well. Actually I think people work harder in America than in Japan. Japanese workers are complaining more and that is why the American economy is going up and the Japanese economy is going down.'

The new contract stopped short of Japan's much-vaunted (and now crumbling) lifetime employment practice, but Toyota promised job security and status in exchange for loyalty and hard work.

NEW START, OLD GROUND

When Gary Convis first laid eyes on the disused General Motors plant, he was not thrilled. 'It was very eerie,' he recalls. Construction on a new stamping plant was under way but except for those workers the place was deserted. He had expected that, but yet . . .

'If you looked out the door as far as you could see, you'd see nothing but a pigeon and a stray cat,' he says with a nod of his head. 'Nobody on the parking lot. The community was kind of dead. No big motels, a few gas stations, it was very bleak because the plant had closed and a lot of people had moved away.'

The plant was located about thirty miles south of Oakland, one of the nation's major ports with facilities for handling large numbers of steel containers, now the prime method of ocean shipment. As a part of GM's assembly division, which handled the building of the full mix of cars of the five divisions of the company, Fremont, as it was called, produced the Chevrolet Celebrity and Oldsmobile Cutlass. The plant opened to high expectations in 1962. Two other GM plants in California once produced cars, one in Southgate, another in Van Nuys, but one by one, through the exigencies of the market and of the company retrenching, all would eventually close.

Convis had reason to have second thoughts about his decision to be in Fremont on that last day of March, 1984. He was assistant plant manager of Ford Motor Company's Lorain, Ohio assembly plant, 'and I was very happy going about my business', when he got a call from a headhunter. The caller said he was trying to fill a job in California, but Convis said he wasn't interested. He went home that night and told his wife, who was from California, about the offer. As they discussed it, says Convis, they both noted that in bleak northern Ohio, with winter winds boring in from Lake Erie, they hadn't seen the sun in three months. 'She said, why don't you call back and find out more about it?'

Fresh from Michigan State University, Convis joined GM's Buick Division and worked for three years in engineering and production before moving to Ford in 1966. Convis had been with Ford for eighteen years, and says, 'I kind of grew up in the Ford organization. I liked it, worked hard and got promoted.' In fact he was the youngest assistant plant manager in the Ford system. But lately Ford had been in a slump, was not paying any bonuses, and a profit squeeze was on. The next day Convis called the headhunter.

He sat through exhaustive interviews in Cleveland with Toyota and GM executives, he recalls. 'At the end,' says Convis, 'they said they were looking for top people, that I was being interviewed for general manager of the plant', a key job in the system. The choice came down to two Americans. Managing Director Tatsuro Toyoda came to the States for the finals.

'It would be difficult leaving Ford, which was a part of my life. I enjoy this business; I think I have a good personality for it,' Convis laughs and shrugs, 'I've got low blood pressure. But I knew I had to commit, once Mr Toyoda was coming over to interview two of us; if I was picked I could never change my mind. The loss of face would be too damaging.

'I didn't want to leave Ford, but I did want to be part of this opportunity. My main motivation, beyond the personal, was that I saw a unique opportunity for an American to make a substantial impact on other American businesses.'

At the Lorain plant, Convis said he tried to work in the usual environment, with difficult union relations, 'not being able to use your resources as well as you could in a more flexible environment. It was kind of frustrating, the inertia that history had created. Also I perceived that the head guys running the company didn't understand the shop floor. They are good people, but they just don't understand what you are talking about, and they can't learn overnight.'

The more he thought about the possibilities the better they looked: 'I thought, here's an opportunity to use your experience. I couldn't look myself in the mirror and say I had turned it down. Bottom line: very few people are going to get an opportunity like this.'

And so, when he was offered the job, he took it. He would be general manager of the NUMMI plant, in charge of manufacturing. 'A lot of people called this an experiment,' says Convis, 'but to guys like me this was no friggin' experiment (he soon recruited several other Americans for the plant). We had cut our ties and we had moved our families.' And it wasn't for a bigger paycheque and bigger perks. 'I went from driving a couple of company cars to driving a rent-a-wreck. We were here out in no man's land. I also had some guys who said "I hope you got a golden parachute or a good guarantee from those Japanese." Very interesting, Toyota doesn't think that way. Basically, if you are coming to work for them, they are committed to you, you don't need to worry about a golden parachute or a job-security clause, because you know, we are going to make it together. I asked some friends who had gone to Japanese companies about this and they said, you don't need one, forget about it. It took a lot of trust.'

There was some urgency in his hiring, because work was under way, preparing the plant for production, a huge investment of time, manpower and effort. There were also some anxious moments once he got on the job. 'During my interviewing, I was kind of led to believe we could almost hand pick our workers. But when I got onto the job I found out it wasn't quite true. We were sending out application forms to all the people who were out here before, and we were going to invite them back for interviews – no seniority carry-over – we would start the company mostly with old GM workers.'

This was a shock to Convis because 'I got to know some of the history of this plant. It wasn't good. I wondered what the hell I had got myself into, because that side of the picture hadn't been exactly rosy. What I knew was that this was one of the worst GM Assembly Division plants. I knew GM had combined some operations from separate facilities and there was in-fighting in the union. There had been about 6,000 people here and there were constant quality problems. Labour relations had been terrible. You throw them together, I thought, and you have a helluva time.'

An experienced labour relations expert says the labour position at start-up 'was a bad situation. Toyota didn't really want the UAW. It took a person of Bill Usery's capacity to put a deal together.' Former Secretary of Labor Usery had worked in labour relations at General Dynamics before his government service. His hiring as a special adviser on labour problems for the new joint venture was an appointment that suited everyone.

The application forms went out to about 5,000 former employees of the Fremont plant in March, 1984, together with a covering letter. The letter outlined NUMMI's need for employees of a particular kind: those willing to contribute to 'an atmosphere of trust and cooperation'. It warned that the new company would not tolerate shoddy workmanship or absentee-ism, a persistent problem in the motor industry. Despite the caveats, about 3,000 applications were returned from the former employees.

The hiring routine was like none these potential employees had gone through before. The ordeal lasted three days, during which they were given simulations of jobs they might be doing in the factory. Even today newly hired Toyota hourly workers are given simple skill tests under the practised eyes of veterans to see if they have the motor skills, the strength and the dexterity to handle tools and to work with the materials they might encounter on the assembly line or in other operations. The Fremont applicants were given written tests, then interviews and group discussions. Once they made the grade to being hired as team members they were given a four-day orientation on the Toyota way of doing things, including the Toyota Production System, the importance of safety, the competitive nature of the auto industry and the rules of conduct.

The supervisory employees first hired were given concentrated instruction at Fremont, with lectures, tapes and demonstrations. Then in small groups of about thirty they were sent to Japan for graduate training. They entered Toyota's Takaoka plant and took on jobs on the line for two weeks, working alongside the regular Japanese employees. Japanese trainers selected for the job were given English language instruction and were assigned to individuals from Fremont, and many of them eventually worked in Fremont with the supervisors – team leaders and group leaders – who had come to Japan.

The idea was to get across Toyota's commitment to build a car at the least cost and with the highest quality. 'To do that you have to have a relationship of mutual trust and respect. How do you measure that?' asks Bill Childs, NUMMI's head of human relations, rhetorically.

The company commitment had to be shown to employees. Examples were not long in coming. An employee who was supposed to check certain welds failed to do it and allowed 380 vehicles to pass with a particular weld uninspected. Some defects were found and all the vehicles had to be reinspected and the faulty ones repaired. It was exactly the kind of problem that the system was designed to obviate. The first failed weld should have been noticed and the line stopped. The cause would be found and corrected and no other vehicle would show the same defect afterwards. Theoretically. A NUMMI official recalls, 'Here was an absolutely perfect employee, really conscientious. But he wasn't trained right and didn't learn the job right. Whose fault is that? He should have checked the manifest, but anyway, the guy said this was the way he was trained. You don't crucify the man.' And so the correction of the problem was to make sure the training was more precise. If Taiichi Ohno had been around to ask his five questions they might have found out more, but the immediate problem was fixed. Says Childs, 'If you have a problem you figure out how to deal with it. You don't try to kill the person who made the error. That is the Toyota philosophy. And of course, everybody learned something from the incident.'

GOALS AND OBJECTIVES

The previous president of NUMMI, Iwao Itoh, who took over in 1993, says that, in the context of Toyota's labour policy, 'it is important to encourage people, give them a positive outlook' and reassure them that they are in a company that wants them to contribute for the long haul. When Itoh arrived at the sprawling set of grey buildings the local folks call 'the battleship' he decided to put his own mark on his presidency and inject that positive note.

'The first thing I did,' he recalls, 'was to paint the ceiling of the plant white. Over thirty-two years it had never been painted and it was dark and dingy. By painting the ceiling the image of the plant completely changed. Everybody noticed it.' So did the accountants. It was a mammoth undertaking, and the bill for this morale booster and motivator was $3.5 million. Itoh smiles contentedly, and says he considers it worthwhile expenditure. The next move was to introduce his own set of goals and objectives in meetings with his staff off site. 'We needed these goals and objectives so everybody would understand, for example, how we could increase our quality level by 10 per cent by expressing it as numbers so everybody could understand.' Some aspects of quality may seem intangible, but the way a perfectly fitted door closes or a certain switch operates are often perceived as measures of quality, and their proper design and installation is measurable. Itoh understood manufacturing and working with people, especially people new to the making of cars. Although he began his career at Toyota in the purchasing department he was soon assigned to the newly established overseas project office, working with Toyota's foreign sales offices. Soon he was made a director of the joint venture in Indonesia that manufactured the body for the first Kijang (it means deer), a slab-sided, no frills (no window glass, no climate control) vehicle that has become so popular there. (Today there is a quite luxurious Kijang model available.) Itoh's company joined chassis from Toyota with locally produced bodies.

After five years of that he was called upon to deal with the Canadian authorities over an expansion that was stalled at the government approval level. At the time, Toyota's Canadian plant was turning out 60,000 Corollas a year and Toyota wanted to add a stamping plant so that its parts supply could be adjusted more closely to production. When local officials were petitioned by Toyota for permission to construct this rather major addition to their plant, permission was slow in coming. The Canadian officials had talked with other car makers and it didn't seem to make sense to them. Recalls Itoh: 'In those days the Big Three were all still in mass production and they would have one big facility for stamping, to supply many plants. It was difficult for them to understand that Toyota wanted to put up a stamping facility at a plant that only manufactured 50,000 vehicles a year. Someone said, 'Well, maybe Toyota isn't telling you an honest story because it would not make common sense to the Big Three." It was out of their range of thinking.'

Itoh explained the Toyota concept behind the need for a stamping plant, and that, seriously, the company was going to shape metal for only 50,000 cars immediately, and to use the new facility for no other purpose. He explained Toyota's just-in-time concept and the ability Toyota had to make needed parts efficiently, in small batches. The approval went forward. When construction started, the project looked enormous because the shop needed to be built high to accommodate the tall presses, and the grading below the shop floor had to be deep to handle the scrap from the presses, which is dropped down, collected, bundled and recycled. So during the construction Itoh had explanatory pictures made and sent them to the officials who approved the plan 'to show that we were telling the truth'. The plant has since expanded – and so has the stamping structure – because now the annual production has quadrupled to 200,000 units a year. A few years ago, says Itoh, the suspicious government official, now retired, told him, 'Now I understand the Toyota way.'

At NUMMI Itoh is concerned about keeping a stable work-force, and a relatively happy one. He takes a stroll through the plant every day on a well-known route, which takes him about forty-five minutes, and he knows many of the employees by name. In the company cafeteria he takes a seat at any table, among the team members, chatting easily with them. They all know him. He tells them, if asked, 'Toyota is not a company that just looks at return on equity. As long as the company produces good-quality vehicles and continues to have a stable profit, Toyota will not close it.' He also has to make the operation attractive to General Motors, since NUMMI is still a joint venture. Though the original agreement with the government was to allow the operation for only twelve years, NUMMI was granted approval for continuation of the joint venture when the first period expired. The Chevrolet Nova, the first model produced at NUMMI, has now been replaced by a sleeker, smaller Prizm and a new Corolla, and Toyota's Tacoma pickup truck has been added to the product mix. With a healthy US car market, workers at NUMMI say they believe Toyota will keep the plant going, despite rumours of Asian financial difficulties.

The shock of the new way of doing things has worn off the early employees of NUMMI, but almost everybody has a story. The flashing *andon* lights and the tinkling musical ditties that signal a line stoppage joined the accustomed clang and clatter of metal on metal, the whump of the presses, the hissing of air guns, the eerie feeling of suspense when the line is halted, all accepted movements of the shop floor symphony. But even in white collar territory, the newly hired Americans had a lot to get used to.

Pat Pineida, recalls the culture shock she encountered after she joined the company. A handsome woman with long black hair, she is now vice-president for legal affairs, but she compares her first year at NUMMI to 'going into the military, having your head shaved and being completely stripped down'. Pineida first joined the company after interviews and meetings with company officials in restaurants and other neutral venues in San Francisco. The job sounded great. It never occurred to her, she now recalls, that she would be working at the plant: 'I walked in the first day, and I suddenly realized this was a blue collar environment.'

For someone from the élite and sophisticated legal establishment of downtown San Francisco, where lawyers are powerful and deferred to, it was a world out of joint. 'Not only was the environment blue collar,' says Pineida, marvelling at the fact that she didn't turn around and walk out the first day, 'but I had to take whatever parking place I could find. And then I had to eat with these burly looking men' in the same cafeteria.

'And then there was the open office. I got an office the first week,' she says. It seemed a small but welcome haven from the encroachment of the shop floor into her lofty world of legalese, permit applications and contracts. 'Then the second week they started knocking down walls, and I thought, "Wait a minute, what have I got myself into . . . ?" I had come from an environment where people made appointments to see me. Now there were people at my desk all day wanting to talk to me, all kinds of people. As a lawyer it was a true culture shock. There was more shock to come – like working on the assembly line among the oil and grease.'

Today she laughs at herself as she describes those early feelings. Now she finds the work 'exhilarating. It was an exciting time for me professionally because we were a very lean organization and if you were skilled and sophisticated you would end up doing a number of things, so much more than routine legal work. Everything that needed to be done, you did it. Today I don't know how to do it any differently, nor would I want to.'

Of course, part of her indoctrination included working on the assembly line and learning about the company from the shop floor level. She also went to Japan for training and put in her time on the assembly line there. 'It sensitizes you to the issues that our team members face,' she has concluded. 'As an Hispanic woman,' she says, someone who is sensitive to cultural nuances, 'I have found that race and gender have never been a problem at NUMMI.' Moreover, she thinks NUMMI has helped to internationalize many of the Japanese staff. She thinks the Japanese who come to NUMMI today are much more worldly-wise than their predecessors. 'After fourteen years here I can tell you the people who come here from Japan are very modern; this company is becoming very global in its outlook.'

Itoh is one of them. He says he had a recent meeting with GM chairman Jack Smith and the two agreed that 'we are not only looking for money and profits, a quick return. GM is concerned, as we are, about the future environment. We have built a bridge between GM and Toyota. It is a very strong bridge, and we cannot stop using it.'

CHAPTER SEVEN
A NEW KENTUCKY HOME

If NUMMI was to be Toyota's laboratory for self-confidence in building vehicles in the United States, TMMK was to become its showcase. Toyota is a company seemingly in love with initials and acronyms, and TMMK stands for Toyota Motor Manufacturing, Kentucky, Inc. The Kentucky plant is located in north central Scott County, near Georgetown, one of those places in America that one takes for granted as a rural backwater, a pleasant place in farming country, too close to Lexington and too far from Louisville to attract much attention. Today Georgetown and Georgetown's Toyota plant is a magnet for job seekers and for tourists. Since the start of construction in 1986, a quarter of a million people have toured the plant. Many of the visitors are from Kentucky, but others have come from as far away as Australia. Scott County officials estimate that the revenues from tourism in the area have jumped from $18.6 million a year to almost $50 million since construction of the Toyota plant began in 1986. If anybody thinks the love affair with the automobile has dissipated they should go to Georgetown, where five days a week tour groups and individuals are rolled through the plant in electric carts on guided tours. A large, open visitor's centre welcomes tourists to the plant at 1001 Cherry Blossom Way. Here the folks can examine the new vehicles being built at Georgetown, play with interactive displays and hear details about the company and the plant operations while they are waiting for their tours to start. The experience is almost like a free visit to a theme park.

When Toyota began searching for a site to build its second manufacturing plant, on the heels of its initial success at Fremont,

California, there were plenty of eager bidders. The state of Tennessee had landed the Nissan plant in rural Smyrna, and made a bid for Toyota. It had a good case, since many suppliers to Nissan would be available to serve Toyota as well; in fact, well over one hundred were available, some of them Japanese companies, too. Ohio, one of the first states to woo Japanese manufacturers with attractive incentive plans, was also in the running. In fact the core of the American motor industry and its suppliers, from steel to rubber, lay in the upper midwestern states – Ohio, Indiana, Illinois, Michigan – so all these states had something to offer. Japanese auto makers moving into the United States chose to locate outside the traditional motor manufacturing cities, to seek less urbanized – and less unionized – populations, Fremont, a special case, notwithstanding. The Chrysler–Mitsubishi operation, Diamond-Star Motors, was located in Normal, Illinois. The Subaru–Isuzu venture set up in Lafayette, Indiana. Honda, the first of the Japanese 'transplants', is in Marysville, Ohio. The Mazda operation was set up in Flat Rock, Michigan, on an old Ford site, which seemed logical for them as Mazda was partially owned by Ford.

Despite Toyota's success with the labour situation in the joint venture in California, the idea of training a workforce that had little or no previous experience was attractive, if a bit daunting. But as Shoichiro Toyoda has said, 'Toyota had discovered that American workers were good workers and could learn Japanese methods'. Toyota would rather teach work methods to a new and apt employee that retrain old-fashioned work concepts and practices out of an experienced one. The best place to find these untrained industrial workers was obviously in rural areas. (The suggestion that the Japanese auto makers seek rural sites because of an aversion to hiring blacks and other minorities is denied by executives at Toyota and other Japanese firms. In fact, at TMMK the present work-force is 13 per cent minority, which is a higher percentage of the Toyota plant's population than of the population at large.)

Shoichiro Toyoda and his executives considered all the possibilities for siting what has to be its major US plant. Why not Tennessee, with its suppliers (and also some Japanese-trained workers)? Toyoda liked Tennessee, he explained. However Toyoda, who would later (1994–96) be a senior spokesman for Japanese business as head of Keidanren, the Federation of Economic Organizations of Japan, was sensitive to the international implications of a move such as this. 'It was a favourable location and Tennessee was accustomed to inviting overseas business. The state government provided fine arrangements as to the land and roads and it looked like a very good location,' he told me. 'But there were many Japanese companies already there in Tennessee and I felt that we had to avoid too much of a concentration of Japanese corporations in one place.'

Kentucky's incentive package, of course, was also a major factor. In fact, it was so favourable that it became a bone of contention in the state. The agreement signed by Shoichiro Toyoda and then governor Martha Layne Collins in 1986 committed the state to some $147 million worth of 'incentives', including $30 million worth of land preparation on Toyota's 1,300 acres. There would be another $10 million for water and gas lines and $12 million for treating the plant's waste water. Kentucky also agreed to make $32 million worth of highway improvements to facilitate the stream of just-in-time delivery trucks with material going into the plant and shipments out of the plant. And the state would pour $55 million into training and education for the employees to be hired. Toyota, on its part, pledged to invest $800 million to build and run an assembly plant that would turn out 200,000 passenger vehicles a year with about 3,000 workers and an annual payroll of $90 million.

There was a lot of scepticism about the deal. Even the editorials of the prestigious *Louisville Courier-Journal* had reservations. The offer to Toyota was the biggest incentive package the state had ever offered. In the gubernatorial election campaign of 1987, one TV spot for Wallace Wilkinson, who won the election, charged that Kentucky's offer to Toyota was much too generous, and made Kentucky 'a laughing stock from Tokyo to Tennessee'. Nevertheless, the state legislature liked the idea and approved the incentive package. Ground was broken in May, 1986. Even before the plant was completed, Toyota upped the ante on its side by announcing that it would add a facility to build 200,000 four-cylinder engines, and the ante kept going up until Toyota had eight million square feet under roof.

The first Camry was driven off the assembly line in May, 1988, and in 1990 Toyota decided to double the capacity of the plant to 400,000 vehicles by adding a second assembly line on which it would build another car, the full-size sedan called the Avalon. It would begin production of the Sienna minivan, built on the basic Camry platform, in 1997. Toyota didn't ask for any more incentives, but financed all its expansion privately. Production bloomed from the original intention of 200,000 cars until, in 1997, Georgetown assembled 325,123 Camry sedans, 80,277 Avalon sedans, and 26,746 Sienna minivans, a total of 432,146 vehicles. Georgetown built the engines for these vehicles, and a few more, plus most of the necessary other components, such as cylinder heads, engine blocks, crankshafts, rods and axle assemblies. In fact, the domestic content that Toyota had estimated to be 60 per cent, rose to 75 per cent.

KENTUCKY'S 'GOOD DEAL'

In fact, the original deal with Kentucky may have been only the tip of the economic iceberg. A new report by a University of Kentucky professor of Finance, Charles F. Haywood, prompted the *Courier-Journal* to run an editorial on 15 October, 1998 headlined 'Good Deal for Kentucky'. The paper recalled its original reservations. 'Like many other Kentuckians,' wrote the editorial writer, looking back at its original scepticism, 'we had reservations twelve years ago about the $147 million in financial incentives that Gov. Martha Layne Collins had offered Toyota to persuade the giant auto company to build a factory in Scott County. That was a lot of money – the biggest such incentive package in Kentucky history. How could we be sure the prize was worth the price? We needn't have worried.' The paper referred to Prof. Haywood's study on the impact of the Toyota deal and concluded: 'That impact has been awesome.' The *Lexington Herald-Leader*, in its story on the Haywood study, agreed: 'Toyota is that rare breed of company that under-promises and over-delivers.'

In short, Haywood pointed out that Toyota proposed to create 3,000 jobs; it created 7,700. The original $90 million payroll now stands at over $470 million. The average income anticipated in the original deal was approximately $30,000; by 1997 the average employee income stood at $61,000. Toyota originally promised to invest $800 million, but has actually invested $4.5 billion.

Haywood estimated that the total money the state would spend over twenty years, including interest on the borrowed funds, was $305 million, but that tax revenues Kentucky would reap over the same period attributed to Toyota's expenditures in Kentucky would be $1.5 billion, yielding, by his reckoning, a return of over 36 per cent to the state.

Professor Haywood attributes the economic success of the Georgetown operation for Kentucky to the goodwill and cooperation that existed on both sides of the deal, and notes that TMMK 'has never made any kind of move that could be regarded as intrusive or as "throwing its weight around". Indeed the opposite has been true, as TMMK and Toyota Motor Corporation have been assiduous in seeking to blend in with and be part of central Kentucky.'

One of the first men Toyota picked to get the new plant into operation was Fujio Cho, who is now executive vice-president for corporate planning. He was one of the long-time disciples of Taiichi Ohno, originator of the Toyota Production System. He was not part of the NUMMI experience, and he didn't give much thought to the labour situation initially. And he was blindsided upon his arrival in Kentucky when local construction unions mounted a campaign to force Toyota to use union labour in construction of the plant. Toyota wasn't even building its own plant, but had contracted it out to Ohbayashi Corp., one of Japan's largest construction firms. Ohbayashi had built other buildings for Toyota and had used both union and non-union workers to do it.

But the construction unions in the region were concerned because this was a big project – at least 2,500 labourers and skilled craftsmen would be needed – and the unions had been ineffective in winning some other big contracts. The main bone in the union throat was the Nissan plant in Smyrna, which was built with largely non-union labour. The unions feared the loss of many jobs if Toyota could build its plant without union labour. And so they began a campaign of lobbying, lawsuits and complaints to Congress. The problem was solved when Ohbayashi agreed to hire all workers through the union hall, whether they were union members or not. When it was over, Cho told the *Wall Street Journal* through an interpreter that the whole brouhaha had been 'a learning experience'. As to union representation in the plants, Toyota executives say they can work with or without unions. They proved the former at Fremont but, of course, that was an extraordinary situation. Japanese unions, however, are ordinarily formed within individual companies, not across industrial categories, and tend to be more cooperative than confrontational, although they sometimes can be tough, as Toyota had learned in 1950.

QUALITY QUEST

Fujio Cho joined Toyota Motor right out of college, where, he quips modestly, his main achievements were as a member of the *kendo* (Japanese fencing) team. At Toyota he was assigned to the team of Taiichi Ohno, even though Cho had no engineering degree or mechanical background. Nevertheless he became expert in putting the TPS into operation. Now, at Georgetown, he was facing the biggest challenge of his career.

It is not difficult to grasp his situation: 'The project itself was a big challenge. One hundred per cent of the people we were going to hire were inexperienced in the auto industry – farmers, teachers, merchants – so we were trying to make something out of 100 per cent amateurs. That was the first challenge.

'Second, what we originally produced was the Camry so, at that time, the Camrys imported from the Tsutsumi plant in Japan were already on the US market. So what would happen when the very first car came off the line in Kentucky? It would be compared with the completed vehicles from Tsutsumi, so what we were challenged to do was to compete against the Japanese Camry from the first car off the American line. Naturally, the US dealers were concerned even before we started production. They started cautioning us that, once you put a product on the market and people start rumours saying that the Kentucky plant Camry quality is not good, all the customers would say they wanted their Camry from Japan, not one built in Kentucky.'

Cho's arrival in Kentucky was to be his first experience with an American workforce on the ground in America. 'I had a lot to study about the United States,' he recalls now. 'How the American people think, how they operate, I didn't know, and so even working with my new American colleagues and friends was a challenge.'

He felt he was coming to the US without enough preparation.

'I asked questions about everything. I removed everything about Japan from my mind and instead I began to look at what was happening in front of me, and I based my thinking on what I was seeing. I kept asking my American colleagues and friends "Why?", and they wondered why I was asking all these "Why?" questions.' Fortunately he had with him an American vice-president for administration named Alex Warren, who had come to Toyota via US Steel and Rockwell International. 'He played the role of teacher at my side. With him I could have a talk once a week or so, and thanks to all those meetings I came to understand the US better.'

Cho was not directly involved in the hiring process at George-town, although he helped to create the procedure through which candidates were finally selected. As Cho says, he feels the basic difference between American workers and Japanese workers is that 'the American people are very good at creating and using tools while Japanese tend to think about how they can do the job, what is the methodology best suited for it'. But he also adds that 'the Japanese people are very good followers. You can force them to wear uniforms, or to exercise. However, in the case of Americans, they are individualistic, and you can't force things on them.'

At Kentucky, Cho knew that quality was going to be his burden. 'From the preparation stage we focused on it, and we did everything we could. We created a standard work process and we educated and trained the people about it, to make sure everybody would work to this process. Then we made all the efforts we could to motivate the people; we wanted to make sure they were strongly determined to become Number One in quality.' Team and group leaders emphasized quality and safety, signs went up, workers were constantly reminded of the goal. The idea was to impress on everybody that each worker had to be '100 per cent responsible before they passed on a process to the next person'.

It was not easy to do, says Cho: 'It took us a little time to make sure this concept took root. Originally, the workers thought that once you stopped the line you would be fired. We had to do away with that idea. I went to the shop floor and said to the employees, "We don't want quantity, we need quality", and what I kept saying was, "You still don't stop the line enough."' For most Americans who understood the conventional concept of mass production and after production repair as traditionally practised, the concept of stopping the line, taking responsibility and participating in a non-accusatory process was still alien.

In the second year of production, TMMK won the Gold Plant Award for high quality from J. D. Power & Associates, the premier automotive rating agency, which makes its awards based upon exhaustive consumer surveys. TMMK has since won two more Gold Plant Awards. Since these awards began in 1990, Georgetown has been placed in the top three six times for vehicle quality.

One of the keys to getting quality, of course, was the kind of people hired to do the work and the supervisors who trained them. The company was flooded with somewhere between 50,000 and 100,000 applications when the word went out that Toyota was hiring. The screening process was exhaustive. Even production workers spent as much as twenty hours in interviews, examinations and testing of one kind or another. *Fortune Magazine* wrote at the time that Toyota gave the top 30 per cent 'the sort of scrutiny that American companies use only for hiring managers'.

Pete Gritton was one of the managers they hired. He is now vice-president of administration and human relations, and he remembers being asked in his interview if he had any questions to ask of the Toyota team that was interviewing him. 'Yes,' he said. 'I'd like to know what your philosophy is about operating with unions.'

'They said, "Well, we don't have a philosophy. What's

yours?"' Gritton was non-plussed by the response. This was at a time when the UAW was trying to organize the Nissan plant in Tennessee. That dispute was bitter, and the issue seemed crucial to him. The Toyota team did not seem concerned. 'They finally said, "We don't see them as good or bad; it depends on the situation." I had never run into that concept before in an American company.'

Toyota wanted to fill the employee relations manager position with a Kentuckian, if possible, and Gritton fitted the bill, as he had experience with one of the largest employers in the state. Says Gritton, 'Basically the philosophy at the start was that Toyota had a system and base of knowledge they were going to teach the Americans to use. The Toyota system would have to be followed meticulously in order to be effective. You can't pick and choose pieces of it; you either do it all or nothing. But human relations is different.'

CULTURES CLASH

The human relations system that worked in Japan, as Cho pointed out, won't necessarily work in the US. 'This was the one area where they would have to adjust to concepts that make sense to Americans and meet American needs,' says Gritton. 'I said we have to go through this issue by issue, policy by policy, and spend time researching what is normal American practice and compare it with what is done in Japan. Then we had to see what combination or hybrid of the two we should put together to support the Toyota Production System. It was a very time-consuming process. We literally would spend hours debating and arguing, sometimes heatedly, about policies and issues.'

One of the first disagreements came over the payment of overtime. The question was whether team members should be paid overtime pay for work over eight hours in the day. US law requires overtime after forty hours in the work week. In most industries, Gritton contended, overtime is paid after eight hours in a day. But the Japanese were against that, largely on the grounds that it would encourage absenteeism, the theory being that a worker who got overtime pay for a couple of days might miss work later in the week because he had earned all the money he wanted. The Japanese staff wanted to pay overtime only after forty hours had been worked in a week.

Gritton said, 'To me this was what every industry does, this is America and I don't know how to justify not paying overtime to a team member after an eight-hour day.' They responded, 'That's not good enough. You have to prove to us that it is the right thing to do.' The debate went on through several long meetings, says Gritton: 'We did deep research and wrote documents outlining the arguments and industry practice in Kentucky, the advantages in terms of team members feeling a sense of fairness. We debated about whether overtime pay on Monday night is really going to affect absenteeism on Friday.' (It is worth noting that overtime at Toyota is mandatory. The team system would simply not work if it were voluntary.)

'I remember a heated meeting we were having one night – we held them at eight o'clock – and I was pacing, walking around the room making my points and arguing. The Japanese had been arguing every step of the way, and I was in mid-stride and mid-sentence and they said, "OK, we'll do it". I wasn't done yet, I had another thirty minutes of material but I sat down real quick so they couldn't change their mind.'

Overtime continues to be a hot issue in Toyota plants despite the absence of the pay issue. *Andon* boards show workers on each shift whether and how much overtime will be required of them on the current day. Georgetown has never had an extended period without overtime. As Gritton puts it, 'We say that because the industry is subject to wide variations of demand, we have to use overtime as one of the ways to avoid overhiring. We want a stable workforce and we don't want to lay people off, reduce work hours and so on, so we use overtime to balance out fluctuation in demand.'

However, the unpredictability of the system does not sit well with American workers and this is also being sensed in the company's British operations. Gritton explains that a worker may be scheduled to finish work at 4:15 p.m., but until they are at work they do not know if they are getting off at their regular time, or at 4:30 or 4:50 or 5:00. 'What I would ultimately like to do is to be able to predict at least a full week ahead, but for now maybe we can do it day by day, at least one day in advance.' Other companies have gone to shorter working weeks and pay for more hours than are worked, as Nissan has done, but this works only in times of slump, and the cost can be unsustainable over the long haul. Toyota tries to find other ways through the problem.

Another time-consuming clash of cultures the human relations team faced at the early stage of construction was the building of changing areas and shower houses for employees in the plant. The first designs provided a simple facility of walls, but no roof, and no rest room facilities, only lockers and shower stalls.

Meetings were called. Gritton says, 'I told them, I know you want to manage costs but you can't do that by not putting toilet facilities in your shower houses. These debates took weeks. They wanted no roof – a roof meant more expense, a special sprinkler system and we would lose flexibility if it was necessary to move the shower houses with a change in plant layout.'

There were a couple of cultural points in this argument that were not understood by the Americans at first. For one thing, in Japan toilet facilities are normally kept separate from bathing facilities. And in Japan until recently, women did not work in the plants. A shower house with no roof is all very well, said Gritton, but with the conveyor line overhead and the possibility of people working up there, it is not a good idea because we're going to have hundreds of women and they are going to want a roof. It took several months of debate to settle that issue in favour of the American system.

Such disagreements were not unusual in the early days of Japanese entry to the industrial scene in the United States. Management expert Peter Drucker once told me of a Japanese client who was confused by America's non-discrimination and equal opportunities laws, and asked whether it would be permissible to have separate men's and women's toilets.

WINNING THE LOTTERY

The concern on the part of Gritton and the entire management is keeping workers happy and productive. They must be doing a lot of things right because a surprising 60 per cent of Georgetown's 7,700 employees each year have a perfect attendance record – at work on time every day. The reward for all those loyal employees is an annual party where the entertainment has been provided by the likes of Dick Clark, David Copperfield and the Beach Boys. But there is another lure. Each year there is a draw at which fifteen of the year's perfect attendees win cars: Toyota donates nine Camrys, three Avalons and three Sienna minivans for the party. The cars go to the winners, with taxes paid.

On-site college courses with free tuition are offered at TMMK, where all the team members have a high school education or the equivalent, more than 50 per cent have some college education and 25 per cent have college degrees.

The suggestion system powered by this educated workforce has been effective. Toyota reckons that since 1989 cumulative cost reductions from employees' ideas have totalled $249 million, $72 million of this in 1997 alone. Team members have devised jigs and devices to make their work flow more smoothly and efficiently, and with less strain. With company engineering help they have devised a caddy seat that allows workers to slip inside a moving car to install interior components without scraping knees or barking shins. Rolling parts carts were devised to cut down on needless walking back to replenish parts as the line moves along. And devices to raise auto bodies to more comfortable levels allow installation of heavy components without back strain. Travelling around the Toyota system one discovers that there are many claims for the invention of these devices, but then there are variations of many of them throughout the Toyota world.

For worker peace of mind, a family centre on the plant site provides professional day care for children of employees for about $70 a month. Toyota donations have built a new high school in Scott County, and each year Toyota awards a high school senior a full four-year scholarship to Georgetown College. Since 1985 Toyota has donated more than $10 million to community and state organizations, including gifts to the University of Kentucky library, and Kentucky Educational Television.

Stories of the impact of the new plant on the lives of people in Scott County are taking on the aura of legend. One of the best comes from Cheryl Jones, a bright and blonde young Georgetown woman who came into Toyota with no notion of what would be in store for her. She graduated from college and came home to Georgetown to go back to the supermarket where she had worked from the age of sixteen. With her new education and skills she rose to be customer service manager, supervising forty people – checkers, baggers and stockers. 'There wasn't a lot of opportunity in Georgetown. IBM was downsizing, and no companies were hiring at that time in Lexington,' she recounts in a soft drawl. Then she heard that Toyota was hiring.

'I dressed up nice for the first interview. Had my nails done and everything. Just about the first thing they asked me was "How do you feel about getting your hands dirty? Working on the plant floor?" I said, "Don't let my nails give you the wrong impression. I've worked on my feet all my life." They hired me as a group leader at the age of twenty-four, took a chance on me.

'When I told them I got hired in a management position at Toyota,' she says with a grin, 'everybody at Kroger's just about fell over. My father is fifty and he could hardly believe all the opportunities they were giving me, because he never had this kind of opportunity. I felt like I won the lottery.'

Within a week she was on her way to Japan, learning about TPS and putting in her time on the assembly line ('you break a sweat in about twenty minutes'). She worked on the line every morning for two weeks with a Japanese trainer who would sometimes slap her on the hand when she made a wrong movement installing grommets in the door plates of Camrys. Back in Georgetown after training she soon found herself a group leader on the trim line, where the cars come in from painting and the first interior insulation is installed. She was the leader of 241 team members and four or five team leaders. The thought of it fills her, even today, with a certain amount of awe. But it was nowhere but up for the tough minded and hard working Jones. She joined a pilot group that went to Japan to work on model changes on the updated Camry, where she learned how to do new model investigation and participate in the prototype development. She also got a promotion to assistant manager of the pilot group. 'We actually set up how to do every single job on every model,' she says. At TMMK she saw the new models up and running and was promoted to manager of Assembly #2 shop, with 800–1,000 team members under her leadership. 'I felt the whole burden of the plant on me,' she says.

Today she is assistant general manager for paint and plastics. Of course she has worked with the spray gun herself, but at first the experienced hands only allowed her to spray wheel wells, where the work could be touched up if she goofed. 'Everybody works hard out there,' she says, nodding toward the plant floor. She considers herself one of them. Her calendar has entries far into 1999. On a date far ahead she will have lunch with second shift team members from 9:45 to 10:30 p.m. Why would she eat with the night shift workers? 'At my last opinion survey (a standard fixture at Toyota plants) one employee commented, "I've been in paint for eight years and I've never seen a manager in my break area", which is the place where they go on break and for lunch. I thought, "Gosh, I don't want that to go on another eight years, so I decided to go out to their break areas and have lunch with them where it's more comfortable for them".' She has scheduled lunch breaks with all her teams.

Jones takes work home by the armload, but still finds time Tuesday and Thursday nights to join other volunteers of the plant's Habitat for Humanity project, which so far has built seven houses for the needy. One recent night she found herself installing door sills. She told her fellow workers on the project, 'I've had my fill of shovelling. I can swing a hammer as well as you guys.' Nobody at TMMK doubts that.

CHAPTER EIGHT
FINE-TUNING THE PRODUCT

On a wall at Calty Design Research is a graphic display of the changing taste of the American auto-buying public since the 1950s. It includes swatches of carpet material, colour chips and even bits of a loud red plaid seat cover material, the likes of which haven't been seen in half a century. This visual history and primer of US automotive taste is a constant reminder of change for the designers who work in Toyota's southern California design research division, a think tank of advanced design and creative design trends. Located in an almost hidden industrial park in swank Newport Beach, Calty is a small but influential link in the structure that helps to create the shapes and images that Toyota vehicles offer in the US market. Calty does in the US what the design group EPOC does in Europe. In between the two, in Ann Arbor, Michigan, Toyota's Technical Center applies further customizing touches and the engineering tweaks and changes needed for cars made and marketed in the US.

Akira Tanaka is a Calty colour designer, one of a design team of twenty, and one of three Japanese on the team who serve as liaison members. (A separate model development team, which crafts new designs in clay and plastic, employs eighteen.) Tanaka notes amusedly that 'Japanese now like more vivid colours, and the Americans like more subtle colours.' Beige, he says, is basic with US customers, but is not popular in Japan. And so part of Tanaka's job is to research different industries, including housing, furniture, apparel and of course the other car makers, to see which way they are leading, or following, American taste preferences. Supervisor Alan Buyze points out the importance of concluding the colour for a design early on, in time for the proper testing to take place – with paint, for example, which has to be given exhaustive durability tests before it can be used in production. The Color Marketing Group, an association of US industries, meets twice a year and members make crucial decisions which set patterns through many industries from household appliances to boats, and years in advance. Says Buyze: 'It's kind of like safety in numbers. If you can get a collective opinion you will get a general idea of where it is going, so no one is sticking his neck out and going in the wrong direction. But somebody might just be going in the new direction.' New directions can be economically dangerous if they aren't backed by good research. One complaint against Toyota's cars for years has been that they somehow seemed dull, unexciting. In the last few years an assault has been made on that front, to give Toyota's offerings a more modern, youthful appeal at one end of the line, and elegance at the top end.

The final decisions on Calty's car designs, interior and exterior, are made after a long and competitive process. Buyze said Calty pulls together the forecasting resources for fabric and paint, then 'we make proposals, and we invite members from Japan and North American facilities to review our selections. We have an evaluation process where we have questionnaires filled out and we get some kind of consensus. Sometimes it supports our direction and sometimes it might be a little different. We have meetings that include the sales and product planning people who are directly related to product.'

The process of design at Calty, says Kazuo Morohoshi, the executive vice-president of Calty, 'starts with a pencil line on paper, and ends with a car on the road'. In an office decorated with simple plain paper abstract sculptures Morohoshi can look out into a green Vista created to seclude the activities in the low, rambling Calty buildings. Those lines on paper are closely held.

Morohoshi takes care to point out that not all the design comes from southern California. There is, of course, the main studio in Japan, and Calty also has a New York satellite studio. Bicoastal visits are frequent because, 'a designer has to know the difference in feeling' between customers in different parts of the United States.

As the design team works closely with the home office in Japan, the liaison Japanese are indispensable, says Morohoshi. 'We know the language barrier still exists, but the interpretation is not only language but also conveys something cultural. That's why we have the three designers here.'

Although Calty has been involved in design for most of Toyota's top sellers in the US market, from the luxury Lexus LS400 to the new Camry Solara and the hybrid Prius production model, it is also useful in training Toyota staff sent from Japan. As Morohoshi puts it, 'One of the philosophies with our establishment is that we have a kind of cultural exchange. The automobile business is now a worldwide business and Toyota's activities are going on all over the world. When people come to work for Toyota they have a new way of life, and the company has to prepare them for the challenges they will now find. We need to educate each other.'

A thoughtful man, Morohoshi says the automobile and its future direction are important for ecological, economic and personal reasons. While 'it is important (for a company) to make a profit, the meaning of the profit is not only money, it is also the attempt to fulfil a dream. Yes, the system is an economic one, the same all over the world. But too much concern about such things can lead to making a money game out of it. We are tired of this. It is boring, just making money – people constantly on the telephone or hunched over the computer, watching the stock market prices change. Our people like to make something, a unique product, an automobile.'

Morohoshi studied industrial design at Chiba University and joined Toyota in 1963, the year before the Tokyo summer Olympic Games of 1964. The Olympics were a kind of watershed in Japan's modern history. It was, in a very real way, Japan's post-Second World War 'coming out', as athletes and visitors from around the world descended on a virtually unknown country. And Japanese had a first hand look at real live foreigners on their soil, could see them in large numbers, acting in their natural national way and often interacting with Japanese. It is difficult to over-emphasize the impact of the Olympics on the urban population. The games stimulated commerce, of course, and industries, including automotive and electronics. Everybody needed a television set to see the games. It was during that Olympic period, says Morohoshi, that Japanese 'understood how many types of people there were in the world . . . everybody understood that the world was not only Japan, there were many people, sportsmen, coming from outside; people in Japan didn't know these other countries and peoples existed.'

At that time Morohoshi was involved in developing the small car called the Sprinter, a model variation of the Corolla, a car that suddenly became the best-selling car in Japan. This car, now after many facelifts and upgrades, is still a top seller. 'I am proud of that,' says Morohoshi.

Toyota sent Morohoshi to the Illinois Institute of Technology in 1969 for graduate study in design, and he took his breaks from school as an opportunity to drive around the United States and see how people lived and what and how they drove. Back in Japan as a key member of the design team he was appointed the general manager of all Toyota design until he was assigned to Calty in 1997.

Today he is an advocate of freedom for designers. But, as he puts it, the design department is part of the technological department, 'so we have to be careful not to have too much freedom'. Because of the economic nature of the business, designers complain, when times are tough, design budgets are cut. In Toyota top management, says Morohoshi, there is an understanding that, although design is a part of engineering, it must also be a part of sales, that it must be independent but it must work closely with these other departments. Designing cars and building clay and big plastic models is an expensive art, and a lot of what is proposed, and paid for, is eventually rejected. Last year, for example, says Morohoshi, 'We were three times in the batter's box, but got no hits.' The reason, he says, is in the nature of the business. In the area of design one is dealing with elusive concepts. 'The idea of image is our responsibility. In many other professional areas it is easy to define activities concretely. But with us it is just image. That is a very challengeable thing and all our members understand it.' Where other engineers talk about 'very realistic things', smiles Morohoshi, 'often our side sounds like it is talking crazy, but it is sometimes necessary. Don't ask us why.'

FITTING IN

Taking those designs that score hits and making sure they adapt to the US market is partly the responsibility of the team at the Toyota Technical Center (TTC), in Ann Arbor, Michigan. In another quiet and secluded campus, the engineers try to make sure that the cars fit the demanding requirements of customers in North America's car culture. Beside performing the emissions certification tests on new models, TTC also put new models through their cold weather tests in Canada. (The hot weather tests are done at a TTC proving ground in Arizona and emissions research for California's higher standards is done in southern California, as well as some dynamic and static vehicle engineering.) Parts and materials suppliers in the US work with Toyota in joint development through TTC.

James W. Griffith is a specialist in fine-tuning cars to local markets. As TTC's vice-president of technical planning he can go through a long list of the changes and adjustments that must be made to make a Toyota car compatible with the American motor scene. For example: 'Take interiors. This is not flippant, but Japanese drive with the steering wheel on the right side and we drive with it on the left and there is a difference in how people feel about it. If you look at me, I have a very significant wingspan.' He opens his long arms wide by way of demonstration. 'And I have a long lower torso and a shorter upper torso. This is not uncommon in Americans compared to Japanese, and it is a big thing. How something feels, a seat, a cushion, is important. I need a long seat and I need to sit higher. The Japanese seat is much lower and much closer (to the wheel), and so we must look at American ergonomics, not just American taste.'

Amenities such as stereo systems, says Griffith, also need fine-tuning for Americans, who like to hear a lot of bass, while Japanese like to have more treble and midrange.

In leather, American taste is now toward a more crumpled. European type of supple leather and a softer seat, while the Japanese seat tends to be firmer. This kind of seat was used in the early models of the Lexus sedan. That car has been given a somewhat softer seat for the US market.

'We drive at high speeds in the United States,' says Griffith. 'I sometimes drive to Chicago going 85 to 90 miles an hour. You don't do that in Japan. So in high-speed driving you need to see certain features on the instrument panel at a mere glance, and it not as necessary to do that in Japan.' He points out that, nevertheless, the instrument cluster in the new Prius hybrid car has been moved higher, more central, and therefore closer to the driver's line of vision, an idea he thinks will be adopted by many auto makers. Head-up displays, which project certain information on to the windshield, as in fighter planes, has been offered by some American manufacturers. It is an expensive system, and one that has not yet appealed to Toyota designers and management, but may appear in some models at the high end of the line.

Americans also like big wheel and tyre sizes, with some cars, such as the Lexus GS400 and the Chrysler 300M, beginning to boast 17 inch wheels. As Griffith puts it, 'It's a look,' but it also tends to cause some slight compromise in handling, and wheel wells have to be made a bit bigger to accommodate them. Of course the turning radius, the distance one needs to turn the car around, is increased as tyres get bigger.

Another favourite topic among car buffs is the noise a car makes. 'Japanese vehicles tend to be very quiet,' says Griffith, 'and I think psychologically Americans think that's not a strong enough sound, so exhaust tuning is becoming more important. My Lexus has a throaty sound to it now.' He shakes his head in mock disbelief: 'The idea of this unbelievably quiet car . . .'

In America the baby boomers are ageing and their children, the eighteen- to thirty-year-olds are the new challenge. Griffith notes that these young people have a strong work ethic. 'They want more money and more free time. They have an entitlement theory. They are not into football or organized big spectator sports. They are more into windsurfing, rollerblading, rock climbing, individual sports. And so someone has to make a point of connection with those people, and design products they love.' This, and the low price of gasoline, helps to explain the emphasis on pickup trucks, minivans and sports utility vehicles (SUVs) of most manufacturers.

Toyota wants to go worldwide with their cars, says Griffith, 'But, instead of having a so-called world car, we are looking at platforms and trying to have similarities in platforms, recognizing that there are differences in local markets. We are trying to have a Camry for North America and one for Japan, and we want them to be as similar as we possibly can from a cost standpoint, but they have to be differentiated. I think this is the direction the business is headed.'

The trends in the way cars are presented to the public continue to change. Griffith points out that, as gasoline prices plunge, that influences the way people think about the kind of cars they want to drive and own. A litre of Evian water costs about 40 cents in the United States. At the end of 1998 in New Jersey gasoline was selling for as little as 92 cents a gallon. Says Griffith, 'My view of history is that OPEC made the market for the Corolla, the Volkswagen, the Tercel. What we are hearing is that, from a trend standpoint, low-end vehicles are suffering, and will for some time in the American market. In Europe it is different.' For one thing, gasoline there is much more costly than water.

They know that very well at Toyota's European Office of Creation (EPOC) at Zaventem, just five minutes away from Brussels airport. Here designers for Toyota are creating new designs for the European market even as the framework of Toyota's newest manufacturing facility rises at Valenciennes, in northern France. The Yaris, Toyota's first entry designed just for the southern European market, has just been introduced to press and public at the Paris Auto Salon in September, 1998.

John McLeod is chief designer of the exterior design department at EPOC and he recalls the challenge of producing the Yaris. 'Basically, it starts from nothing; all that was said to me was that it would be the next entry car for Toyota. What we needed was a small car.' He liked being given the challenge. Having worked for British and French firms, 'I thought there ought to be some more efficient ways of working than that, where 95 per cent of what you do you can throw in the bin three months later. You see very little of what you do translated into sheet metal. It is very frustrating, stressful.'

And so the Yaris project began with a blank piece of paper. As McLeod explains it, 'We knew we had four people to fit into a certain space. Sounds simple but you have to work out the seat height or the relationships to the gas pedal and to the windscreen, or whatever, but basically we start with the people. We need a certain amount of trunk space or boot room. We wanted to be better than other cars in that segment in terms of space and hopefully in terms of styling, and certainly in terms of having a little more elbow room, leg room or head room. So basically every time Toyota makes a car we want it to be better than the other cars.'

Obviously, the inherent problem in designing small cars is that they are small, he concedes, and McLeod, who stands 194 centimetres tall, is certainly one to appreciate size. As engines have become more compact, he points out, 'a small car is not just four seats and some wheels. A lot of small cars don't pay enough attention to leg room, head room or storage space. It is a big plus factor to have these items attended to in a car,' and that is the direction the EPOC team went with the Yaris.

Furthermore, the small car in Europe has a different image from the small car in Japan, or even America, he says, 'It is not just a low-budget, low-income kind of car, so we figured we needed some kind of quality as well as comfort.' And, although the main target audience is young people, the idea was to make it acceptable to older people as well. And so, instead of lowering the roof line, the team raised it. This is partly the result of market research and buyers' preferences, as well as sound engineering decisions. While the Yaris was in the early stages of development, focus groups were evaluating designs and telling investigators their gripes, complaints and likes about Toyota and other cars.

The design team sent a full-size model to Japan, and got approval to go ahead with the project – but not for the full-size model they had sent. Says McLeod, 'They could see the proportion, height, width, but it was nothing like the resultant car. It's OK. In the first model the goal is to win the project; it doesn't matter about styling in the first stage. The designer, of course, wants it to go his way immediately, but as you go on, someone is going to say, "yeah, great product but terrible styling. Do it again." That is normal in the first stages.' As it worked out the winning designer was Sotilis Kovos, and everybody rallied around his design.

Kovos, at the introduction of the car, said he felt it was important that customers 'feel there is something in front of them to emphasize safety. My proposal was always designed to create the effect of a big volume at the front of the car.' This yielded a broad expanse of metal, giving, the designers hoped, a feeling of strength and quality. Kovos said he thought the car does not have national characteristics. 'Yes, the European influence is dominant,' he agreed. But 'harmony and maturity are the key words. The Yaris is an attractive car but I did not set out to make a cute car.'

The new higher rooflines seem now to be a trend, says McLeod. 'If you go to the cars from the 1930s they were incredibly high. People were wearing top hats, cars were enormous, roads were bad. Cars in the 1940s got lower and longer, and in the 1950s wider and even longer. In the 1970s downsizing began and the general size of cars goes in fashions. Right now the fashion is to get shorter, wider and the new trend for compact cars is to get higher. I think we at Toyota are right in the trend.'

Yet the cars have to look good; if they look 'funny' they won't sell, because, opines McLeod, 'at the end of the day they don't buy for functional reasons. They buy on emotional reasons.'

As at Calty, EPOC bids with the home office for which cars it wishes to work on. 'Toyota is a very big company,' says McLeod, 'and every year ten new cars are in production, so our director, when he goes to Japan, he can see the timing and choose the projects he would like to do. He makes his proposal to the design manager in Japan.' Sometimes he gets the projects he wants and brings home new challenges for the sharp pencils of his staff.

At EPOC, as at Calty, they have computers and software for computer-aided design, but these are not the centre of the designer's attention. As McLeod puts it, 'You can draw something on the computer, if you are very skilful, but you can do a quick pencil sketch in five minutes. Designers are so used to making a fast small sketch, just a few lines quickly. If you spend too long on a drawing it becomes laboured, too "designed". Some very quick first sketches are very useful.' He shrugs, contemplating the pencil–computer disconnect: 'A car designer is just a car designer. Very narrow minded, perhaps.'

CHAPTER NINE
TRUCKING IN INDIANA

When they needed someone to head Toyota's new truck plant in the United States, they turned to a veteran of plant start-ups and production engineering named Seizo Okamoto. An alumni of the Ohno era, he helped to install the Toyota Production System at NUMMI, and did the same at TMMK under an old mentor, Fujio Cho. When Indiana was selected as the site of the newest Toyota assembly plant, Okamoto, a personable and talented engineer, was a logical choice.

Nearly twenty years ago Okamoto was sent to Long Beach, California to apply TPS to a company that was producing truck beds to be joined to Toyota truck cabs shipped over from Japan. As Toyota officials in Tokyo simplify it: they wanted to export trucks to the US, but the tariff on trucks was a hefty and prohibitive 25 per cent. However, the duty on an uncompleted truck, such as a cab and chassis, was only 5 per cent. The solution, then, was to ship only incomplete vehicles to Long Beach and fit the truck beds to them before offering them for sale.

Takeshi Nagaya, now president of Toyota Motor Corporate Services of North America (TMCS), had been sent to the US in 1971 to find a company to build the truck beds. He settled on a small firm called Atlas Fabricators, based in Long Beach. They produced shells for torpedoes for the navy and other military parts and had, as he recalls, 'Just enough equipment and know-how to produce a truck bed.' By the end of the year Atlas later to be called Long Beach Fabricators, then TMM, and then TABC, was shipping truck beds to the ports of entry that received the cabs.

'This was the first application of TPS in the US,' says Okamoto. 'TABC was the company. They were producing stampings and parts for the truck beds. The way they operated was that supervisors would go to the warehouse in the morning and check the parts and decide what parts would be produced. The idea was to keep the warehouse full. The stamping process was completely independent. What a complicated process they had! After stamping one large lot of parts, it would go into inventory. The next day they would go on and make a large amount of another part.' Okamoto set up a just-in-time system so that there was no overproduction of parts, thus reducing the inventory. He put in place 'a so-called production line', as he calls it, which integrated several processes, and smoothed the flow of work by applying the *kanban* system. Then he went to work on the assembly system and reorganized the paint shop. Today, he says, 'TABC is a model TPS plant.'

'At first, the workers were very doubtful,' he recalls. 'Nobody understood the purpose of this change. TPS was unknown to them. This was 1979. When they saw the results of what we were trying to do, they started to accept the system and they became very cooperative.' Today TABC is wholly owned by Toyota and produces truck beds for the NUMMI operation, as well as stamped parts and catalytic converters.

On the heels of that success, Okamoto was tapped to coordinate the body assembly division at NUMMI. It was a major challenge for him, by then a newly appointed manager. At NUMMI it was difficult to maintain a smooth production flow at first. The workers were stopping the line often, as they were instructed to do when anomalies occurred, but getting the required production was difficult. Operating properly, the line does stop and the musical signal echoes through the plant, but those stoppages become fewer and fewer as the new assembly crews gain experience. The projected assembly target was to maintain 95 per cent availability. Says Okamoto: 'We set the conveyor speed at one minute a car, or sixty per hour. If we got sixty cars in that hour we would have 100 per cent availability. It takes a long time to get high availability. I wanted to reach 95 per cent availability for at least one day, just to show our members we could do it.' Team leaders and group leaders were drilled on responding to the *andon* calls quickly and sizing up the problem as fast as possible in order to make a correction. Okamoto was there on the line every day, encouraging them, stepping in when necessary with a team or group leader. NUMMI started production in December, 1984, says Okamoto, 'and in May we hit 95 per cent. We celebrated that day.' The symbolism of that 95 per cent was significant, he points out, because it gave everybody confidence. Toyota also gained confidence with NUMMI that they could do good work in the US.

After two years at NUMMI, Okamoto went back to Japan to work in body engineering, and was named vice-president of engineering at TMCS. In his new job he was overseeing production engineering plans for further US production. 'I had to be involved in all kinds of areas – plant construction, environment, machining, boring, casting, plastics, paint, stamping, styling – I was very busy,' he recounts. The focus was on Kentucky and the crucial first stand-alone integrated Toyota plant in the US. Okamoto had 150 members on his team. When his division was consolidated into what is now called Toyota Motor Manufacturing North America, Inc. and located in Erlanger, Kentucky, across the river from Cincinnati, he moved his office there, bought a house and went back to Japan on a one-week business trip in March, 1996.

In the elevator at Toyota headquarters the first morning he ran into a friend. Akira Takahashi, now an executive vice-president, who as a director oversaw preparations for local manufacturing operations in North America. Takahashi casually asked Okamoto, 'Have you heard about it yet?' Okamoto looked at him blankly, obviously not privy to any special news. Takahashi said, 'You are assigned to be president of TMMI.' It was a pleasant shock for Okamoto: being appointed head of Toyota Motor Manufacturing Indiana was a weighty promotion. He extended his Japan trip, met with president Okuda and chairman Toyoda, called his wife and cancelled the house purchase in Cincinnati. Then he looked for Princeton, Indiana on the map.

He found it in near Evansville in the lower left-hand corner of Indiana, a place of flat farmland bristling with corn and soybeans, not far from the Ohio River. By May Okamoto was ensconced in a rented condominium in Evansville, forty miles up Route 41 from the plant site, and on 8 May ground was broken for a $700 million plant. The original giant plant would soon be expanded by nearly half, to a staff of 2,300 and an investment of $1.2 billion.

Toyota had entered the full-size pickup truck market, but plans for TMMI operations shifted when Toyota's offering, the T-100, bombed on the market. Though it found a niche, sales were not brisk enough to suit the Toyota management. American buyers told the survey teams that they wanted a heftier, more powerful truck with a V-8 engine and the capacity to haul and tow more than the T-100. So Toyota produced one. Long accustomed to building the sturdy and dependable Land Cruiser, which found favour with safari guides and hunters in Africa and in the Arabian Desert, the platform could serve as a solid and tried base for a tough truck, and perhaps even a very large SUV.

It was to be named the T-150, but the staff at TMMI, where it would be built, were ambivalent about the name. Okamoto weighed in with a caution: 'Our team members found it too similar to the F-150 [a Ford offering]. I suggested that if you are going to give it a numerical name, make it T-2.' The word came back from Toyota City that the name would indeed be changed: the numbers would be dropped. The new name would be Tundra. 'For Japanese, Tundra has a good sound, very cold and forbidding. I was surprised to learn here that not many people know the word,' says Okamoto.

People in this corner of Indiana had heard of Toyota, though,

Along Tulip Tree Lane, where TMMI now stands, some residents put up signs of welcome before the plant was built. One of them read 'We Welcome Toyota to Indiana'. The well-wisher? The United Auto Workers Union, which has, at this writing, not yet made a major recruiting drive on the new plant. At the rear of the plant site, a local resident put out a sign reading 'Welcome Toyota. Let's Do Lunch'. The name Tulip Tree Drive was chosen in a contest for team members. The tulip tree is the state symbol and, taking advantage of the symbolism, the folks at TMMI suggest that the deep roots of the tall tulip tree represent TMMI's roots in Gibson County.

When Okamoto arrived he couldn't find a suitable place to live in the small town of Princeton, nearest to the site. The company agreed that the best thing to do was to build a company house there for the TMMI president. It is not really surprising that, despite its enormous investment in the production facilities, or because of it, the head office would quibble about the cost of the boss' modest house. After all, the Aichi penchant for frugality and a phobia about wasted resources has been constant in the corporation. 'Budget was always a problem,' says Okamoto with a grin. 'The house was either too big or too small. It took months to get approval.' Until the house was finished Okamoto lived in a condo in Evansville, a forty-minute commute. He and his wife, Tomoko, are in their house now, and are apparently very pleased with it, though Okamoto spends most of his time at the plant, as one might expect.

'The plant is a unique situation,' he says, 'because everything here is new – new facilities, new product, new team members.' But even more important is that the product is also new. No Tundra or equivalent product is being made at any of the Toyota plants in Japan or elsewhere, so TMMI is on its own. 'This is the first production of the truck in the world,' says Okamoto, 'and we have asked for some trainers from Japan to work with our new crew.'

For his part, Okamoto is on the plant floor constantly. During the run-up to production he lectured the supervisory staff frequently on the basics of the Toyota Production System, 'and about my commitment to TPS. I speak to all the new members by myself, personally, welcome them to TMMI, find out who they are, where they come from. I talk about the need for cooperation. I encourage them to come to me at any time with questions, suggestions, or just to talk. Because "open communication" is not just a saying; it is the cornerstone of TMMI.'

A GREEN WORKFORCE

There was considerable initial nervousness because TMMI was a true start-up operation, that is, starting with a totally green crew. But Okamoto says he prefers people with no vehicle production background because they haven't had a chance to pick up any bad habits on somebody else's production line. To help him Toyota has managed to recruit some first rate talent on the managerial side. Among them are the following. Don Dees, a former General Motors production manager and now an expert on TPS, who worked with Opel in Europe, is general manager of manufacturing and quality planning. Norm Baffuno, a former assistant plant manager at GM's assembly plant in Wisconsin, is general manager of production. And Tom Suter, a human resources specialist, is general manager of administration.

Because of its newness TMMI is a good example of the kind of training new recruits go through. It puzzled a lot of local folks that the process took so long. Jacqueline Sexton, manager of human relations at TMMI, who was transferred from TMMK to work on assembling a workforce, found herself virtually alone as the construction started, with Okamoto and a half dozen others. The buzz was heavy in Gibson County as the work progressed on the site, and when the word went out that Toyota was accepting applications, the flood began. Sexton says the preparation of the application forms took months. 'Then, the first week, in late August, 1997, we received something like 30,000 applications' for the 1,300 jobs soon to be available. 'We knew the response would be so strong that we set up sort of a blitz.' Applications centres were staffed at Roberts Stadium, Evansville, at Princeton High School, and at National Guard armouries in Jasper and Vincennes. Fortunately for Sexton and her skeleton crew, the Indiana Department of Workforce Development served as the employment service, to accept and screen the applications. Says Sexton, 'There were lines, people were waiting at the doors every morning; it was like a rock concert.' And it was not as though the area was in a job slump. Unemployment was running at around 2.5 per cent, which is low, even by Japanese standards. Some people applied for a job hoping to earn more money or work closer to home, or for many reasons that Sexton and her crew were interested to hear. Some applied just for the hell of it, as one man put it, some out of old-fashioned curiosity. Few if any knew what was in store for them. The state computerized the applications. The number soon grew to 50,000.

Dealing with such a large pool of applicants was difficult. The potential employees were called to report in groups. Toyota and the Indiana DWD worked together to do the initial assessment. 'We called them in in a truly random way,' says Sexton, though the people living within fifty miles of the plant were given preference. 'The applicants for tool and die makers and maintenance workers were first given a reading and math test. To yield 500 hires we have to test 5,000 at least. Most people do not make it through the initial assessment process.'

The first test normally given is what she calls a 'career fit test'. It is a judgement test. 'We are looking for people who are going to enjoy to work in a new environment. We try to determine how comfortable will they be (in the job situation) and will they share values with Toyota?' Admittedly this is a pretty difficult thing to assess, but Sexton says the tests are 'validated instruments' and so far seem to have worked well in aiding the hiring process. 'The test gives you a situation, asks what you would do in that situation, and provides multiple choice answers.' Or there are simple tests of people's preferences and attitudes. A series of questions asks for reactions to statements such as 'I think it's important to work every day' or 'I feel comfortable talking about . . .' or 'I think quality is somebody else's job.'

Those who make the grade go to a skills test, where they are actually handed tools such as air–powered torque wrenches and instructed in how to carry out tasks with them. They are tested on their ability to participate in a group and not take over, and are given a test to see if they have the ability to identify problems.

As this suggests, the process is exhaustive; it is not as though Toyota are looking for warm bodies to screw bolts on nuts endlessly and mindlessly. The first test takes four hours; the skills tests takes another four hours. This is followed by a day of work, an actual eight-hour day. 'It is not like working on the line,' says Sexton, 'but a simulation. There are physical jobs they have to do, and the question is whether they are physically able, whether they can follow through, check quality and identify problems that occur.' During the testing period the examiners are looking for applicants with leadership ability, who might qualify as team or group leaders.

In the evaluation the candidates are physically tested in what is called 'work conditioning', which includes tests of their flexibility, strength and adaptability. They are given exercises in stretching and movement and sometimes step onto the treadmill or the stationary bicycle for cardiovascular testing. The work simulation involves the pace of plant work, testing the ability of the candidate to accomplish certain tasks. They are helped with demonstrations of how to make physically demanding twisting and bending movements they will encounter in the plant, and do them with ease. Each movement, not surprisingly, has been thought out ergonomically, for the most output with the least effort.

The next step is an interview, after which a successful applicant joins the 'active consideration pool'. This takes longer than the assessment, but even when a 'preliminary job offer' is made it is not the final step. The applicant must go through a physical examination at Gibson General Hospital, which includes a drug test, and if he or she passes they are placed in a job that TMMI chooses.

'We don't intend for it to be intimidating,' says Sexton of the process. 'We want to make sure people have every opportunity to do their best. It is not our intention to try to fail a bunch of people; it's our philosophy that we want them to succeed. We tell our people to make sure not to be offputting. Whether the applicants pass or fail, we want them to walk away feeling good about Toyota, because if they fail that may be the last contact they have with us. We don't want people out there saying, "Oh, they are ugly." Besides, they are going to have friends or relatives working here. People have invested quite a bit emotionally in the process and we want them to know we appreciate their interest in working with us.'

The highest failure rates are on the written tests and the skills tests. Says Sexton, 'At the beginning we show them a videotape that describes who we are and we show them the different areas of the plant – stamping, welding, painting, and so forth – and a couple of team members from Georgetown talk to them about what it is like. We tell them we understand this is not the right fit for everybody and if they choose not to go on we understand.

'A certain percentage of the population that see Toyota have the image of high tech; they think they'll be operating some computer. But we're building cars; there's paint flying around and you have got to put a bumper on that car every so many minutes. If that reality doesn't sink in until it's too late; they're here and they will say, "Migosh, I'll be working in a *factory*!"

'Well, we think it's the best factory in the world, but it's a factory, and that is not what everybody wants to do. Some say, "If this is what I'll be doing, this is not what I had in mind." '

Manufacturers are relying more and more on objective selection processes, skipping the long interviews, but not Toyota. TMMI interviews can last two hours. Sexton says, 'I don't know anybody who does it like we do; it could be overkill. It is expensive to do what we do, and takes a lot of time and a lot of commitment. But after all, hiring somebody is a million–dollar investment for us. We are talking about somebody who is going to stay with us ten years or more, and actually, it could be more than one million dollars.'

Getting everybody on the team is of course a Toyota goal. An extra reminder of the shared experience is the requirement for wearing the company clothes. New members are issued six uniform sets of shirts and trousers or blouses and slacks or skirts, blue and/or white, and they wear them in any combination. The garments are made of fire resistant cotton twill. The buttons are made of rubber and the trousers and skirts close with Velcro instead of a buckle, to avoid scratching the cars. The company name, of course, is stitched on the garments, as well as the person's chosen name. There is also a shop in the plant where other garments, such as windbreakers, can be purchased.

All new members are expected to read and understand the litany of goals, values and mission that are a part of every Toyota operation. The mission: 'As an American company, contribute to the economic growth of the community and the United States. As an independent company, contribute to the stability and wellbeing of team members. As a Toyota group company, contribute to the overall growth of Toyota.'

The goals of TMMI: 'Produce the number one vehicle(s) in the country in terms of customer satisfaction of quality, cost and timeliness of delivery. Maintain steady growth and competitiveness, which will motive team members to take pride in their company and accomplish creative and continuous improvement. Maintain high corporate ethics and reliability with all business partners and society as a whole.'

The values needed to reach these goals include respecting other team members 'by maintaining safety, fairness, participation and improvement'. They urge every employee to be fair, to encourage everyone to participate. They are also expected to comply with company operating philosophies about TPS and promoting constant improvement, or *kaizen*, to practise open communication and mutual confirmation, and finally to 'maintain broad-range thinking and long-term planning'.

This is pretty heady stuff for people who are going to be putting bumpers on trucks, wielding a paint sprayer, or cutting a die. But it is Toyota's way of showing everyone that it is serious about participation. Some old auto line workers find the whole thing objectionable, since it blurs the line between labour and management, which traditionally is conceived as a confrontational relationship. This attitude has changed over the years, particularly since the invasion of the lean Japanese productions systems, led by Toyota. As Detroit companies suffered loss of market share and profits in the 1970s and 1980s, labour was forced to give back some of the financial and other advances they had made over the years. And as workers at NUMMI learned, getting the jobs turned out to be more important than clinging to old systems.

Jacqueline Sexton says team members may have personal and performance problems that the human relations staff have to deal with. 'We try to facilitate the problem-solving process,' she says, 'but we can't fix the problems for them.' One of the challenges the new employees face is that 'they are coming in with experience in all kinds of different companies, and all of them have different ways of doing things, policies and philosophies. And Toyota's philosophies are really different. The way we do things is different from ways other companies do them. It takes a bit of time for people to learn what kind of company Toyota is and what we want it to be. We try to set up systems and foundations for what kind of company we will be, but then it is really up to the team members.'

TMMI workers are given reading materials that say the Toyota Production System 'cannot be accomplished without the ideas and continuous improvement of each team member. Team members need to understand this link and believe that if TMMI is successful they will be successful.'

But if workers are to be truly involved 'they must understand the company's direction and targets'. TMMI has pledged to communicate the targets at all levels, and 'progress and results will be reported so that everyone continually understands the current situation of the company. It is the company's responsibility to tell team members what is going on and to give them the information necessary to both understand and do their jobs.' Conversely, it is each team member's responsibility 'to give feedback to his or her supervisor . . . and to confirm that what they communicate is fully understood'.

This folksy, almost small-company approach to sharing information is accepted as normal at Toyota but was long anathema to giant American auto companies. It sits well in rural southern Indiana. Toyota has tried to be a good neighbour. A Toyota executive visited the man who wanted to 'do lunch' – and took him to lunch. The company turned over 125 unused acres behind the plant to the Future Farmers of America club from Princeton High School and its thirty-some members. The students planted the land with soybeans and have harvested 40–50 bushels an acre. So far they have managed to buy an $8,000 combine with the profits from their work.

Of course, there were dissenters when TMMI was being granted concessions by the State of Indiana and local officials, but there was no outcry as at Georgetown. For one thing it didn't happen in the middle of a political campaign, and Hoosiers had the example of Georgetown, Kentucky to point to, with TMMK's good reputation as a corporate citizen. TMMI put out a quarterly magazine that was distributed widely to tell local citizens what Toyota was doing on its site. It contained news stories about progress during the construction, information on hiring, comments from early hires, and each issue contained a warm message from Okamoto. In his column he wrote about the company goals and progress, he talked about his wife and his children, about their road trips, about rooting for Michigan because his daughter Natsu was a senior there, and he told of unpacking in his new home, when it was finally completed and, just like you and me, trying to find his misplaced golf shoes.

CHAPTER TEN
EUROPE: GIANT STEP

Hiroshi Okuda strode into Takeshi Nagaya's office one day in 1988 with a newspaper in his hand, agitated by what he had just read. Okuda was the Toyota director in charge of the overseas project division at the time, and he had just read a story that said Toyota was lagging behind Honda and Nissan in European operations. 'Aren't you upset by this?' he demanded.

Nagaya's reaction was defensive: 'I thought, it's not my fault. But I studied the situation, and I couldn't find any reason why Toyota couldn't be successful in Europe. So I tried very hard to make a proposal.'

A few days later, at an investment seminar at the British Embassy in Tokyo, Nagaya cornered the commercial counsellor and asked him what his government's reaction would be if Toyota wanted to come to the United Kingdom to produce vehicles. In two weeks the British diplomat called back and said the government would welcome such a move. Actually, Europe was not altogether unknown territory to Toyota. The company began shipping cars to Denmark as early as 1962. A Portuguese manufacturer began producing Toyota vehicles under licence in 1971, and Toyota was producing its fork-lift trucks with a French partner, Manitou, in France in 1987. In 1989 Toyota entered a joint project with Volkswagen to build a small Toyota pickup truck in Germany. The company was selling more than 400,000 cars and trucks a year in Europe – 540,000 in 1998 – despite a crazy-quilt of national import restrictions. A decision to build in Europe would be directly in line with the company's announced policy of building vehicles where the customers are. But full-scale production on its own, rather than a partnership, would mean a heavy commitment of manpower and money. An assembly plant and an engine plant would eventually cost nearly £1 billion, which would be the biggest outside industrial investment in British history.

It looked like it would be a pretty hard sell in Toyota City. Nagaya says his staff told them they had submitted proposals 'many times' in the past. 'They laughed at me,' says Nagaya, 'but I said, "Well, just let me try."' To his staff members' surprise there was a lot of support for the move. His chief supporter, of course, was Okuda, who was then in charge of finance, and who had the confidence of the Toyoda family, whose members were the executive backbone of the company and had the power to say yes or no. Tatsuro Toyoda, then vice-president in charge of overseas, supported the proposal, and his brother Shoichiro, pleased by the NUMMI and TMMK projects, if not by their lack of profitability, gave the all important green light for the project. And so Toyota began searching for a site.

PEEWITS AND PRODUCTION

Mrs Margaret Littlejohn remembers when the news broke that Toyota would come to Derbyshire in the middle of England, into her very own district. In fact she was at a District Council meeting that evening.

'I suppose there were about fifty people in the room,' recalls the emphatic Mrs Littlejohn. 'Twenty-five people groaned and twenty-five harrumphed, and I was one of those who said, "Yes, we've got to make it work."' She was only half of the family, but she was the one with the vote on the Council.

Her husband, now deceased, didn't agree. 'He was an avid bird watcher, a life member of the Royal Society for the Protection of Birds, and he said "You've got to stop it, Marg! You've got to stop it! What about the lapwings, what about the peewits?"'

Peewits, indeed. Fears of vanishing migratory birds were only the half of it. Plant opponents evoked images of vast piles of industrial waste, airborne paint that made some people fearful that 'we were all going to end up with green skin'. But eventually Toyota would come to South Derbyshire. On to the lovely rolling land, to a giant expanse of green, part of which was the former RAF aerodrome known as Burnaston, named for the nearest town, which became Toyota's new address in Britain.

It was not easy. For one thing, there were three places in England under consideration for the assembly plant. The Derbyshire councils involved kept the negotiations with Toyota secret for as long as possible and brought the local press into their confidence on the promise of earliest news of the decision.

Says Robin Gray, a distinguished grey-bearded gent, who was a member of the District Council at the time, 'At first we knew it would be a manufacturing plant for vehicles. We didn't know much detail. We knew it was big; we knew it was an international company.' He also knew that two other areas were bidding for the plant. The package the local councils put together included acquisition of the land, changes to infrastructure to the site boundary, and support with community relations, education and housing. The county council put in £4.5 million toward infrastructure, such as electricity and water facilities. With an eye to future expansion Toyota nearly doubled the size of its site requirement, from 300 acres to 580 acres, which forced the council to buy some private farmland. It is widely believed that the British government completed the new A50 road which makes a crucial road link between the Toyota site and its engine factory in Deeside, North Wales, as part of the deal, though there is no official confirmation. In any case, the link was completed and Toyota trucks carrying the engines for Burnaston's 220,000 annual output of cars rolled along this route.

The Toyota plan attracted about ninety serious objections, says Gray, and a public hearing was held. The plans were on view, explained and debated. As Gray recalls, 'There was a degree of concerted opposition but it was limited to those people who had specific concerns, who either lived close and thought they might be adversely affected, or who had a direct interest in the land, for example a local farmer who owned most of the farm we were acquiring. Or there were some special interest groups such as the Ramblers Association, and the Council for the Preservation of Rural England, concerned at the loss of countryside and the impact of the project. We recognized that there would be problems but, on balance, we felt it was justified.'

It wasn't all opposition, of course. A majority was eager for this economic injection. The region was in a slump that had began when in 1988 the last of the coal mines closed in South Derbyshire, with the loss of about 1,000 jobs. Also, the headquarters of British Coal and British Coal Research and Development, which employed over 1,400, shut down under the Thatcher government's policy of privatization. 'There were quite major structural changes taking place in the economy when Toyota arrived,' says Gray. 'To us it was a godsend, Toyota coming. It had immediate short-term benefits during the construction period and quite clearly it is going to have very long-term benefits, not only through its presence here now but potentially for long-term expansion, and the attraction of local businesses. The confidence that this has brought to the area, to local business, chambers of commerce, local authorities, is incalculable. Suddenly you have this small area in the middle of England that is on the international map, not through its own doing but because a major international company suddenly appears on the scene.'

And so Toyota chose Derbyshire and the new company, TMUK, allayed many fears by planting 350,000 trees around the plant site, and by developing surface water fields to preserve some of the wetlands habitat for the lapwings and the peewits and the swans. The plant was built to minimize noise; the paint shop was built with emission standards ahead of government regulations. From the beginning of construction, no ozone-depleting CFCs or organic chlorides were used. The paint is water-based. The plant boasts that 99.9 per cent of its parts packaging is reused. Waste water is recycled, exhaust gases are used to pre-heat other processes. Complaints there were. The sheer size of the plant interfered with TV reception for some homes, and the BBC was persuaded to relay their signal into the area from another direction.

In order to keep abreast of, or ahead of, citizen concerns, Toyota officials meet with local Parish Council representatives periodically to exchange information and discuss issues of mutual interest. The company has been generous with its contributions to arts and educational centres in the area and the National Trust's environmental education program. And Toyota employees are encouraged to participate in community activities.

'It was a long two years,' says Mrs Littlejohn. But despite anguished complaints that the grass verges of the local roads are being eroded by an increase in traffic, more people are driving – commuters who work at Toyota, and new residents and their cars – and of course the stimulated economy of Derbyshire means more commercial traffic on the road. The flying club has been moved to another site, a disused Ministry of Defence base is being converted into a shopping area and there are plans for 1,700 new houses and a school. 'If I could wave a magic wand,' says Mrs Littlejohn, 'I would stop the erosion of the green verges. It is a real pain,' she says. 'But for sleepy little South Derbyshire, Toyota has woken us up.'

LEARNING CURVES

If the plant was a curiosity to the local residents, who rushed to apply for jobs there, it was a learning experience for those who ran it.

Soon after full-scale production began, Takahiko Yamamoto stood by the assembly line watching team members installing rear glass in an Avensis car. 'I noticed they had some problem,' says TMUK's deputy managing director. 'Fitting the rubber around the glass was difficult, and sometimes the rubber looked wrinkled or wavy, so they were struggling with it.' Yamamoto was always looking for problems to solve. An engineer experienced in virtually every facet of the manufacturing side of the business, he was sent to Kentucky ten times to work with the staff during the start-up. When he was assigned to TMUK he was apprehensive, as most Japanese have become over the years, by the constant reference in Japan to the 'British disease', which is said to be UK labour's penchant for strikes and aversion to hard work. 'I thought that maybe English people are idle,' says Yamamoto, 'but actually, to be frank, I found right away that is not the way it is at all.'

On this day in Burnaston he stepped in and said to the team members on the line, 'Please teach me how you do this.' As the car bodies came down the line he worked with the crew and helped them to install windows on ten cars. Before he was finished he had worked out a way to fit the gaskets smoothly around the glass. 'This is my way of approaching a problem,' says Yamamoto. 'I told the crew that, if there is some concern, some problem, you should share the difficulties. Sometimes it is not very difficult, sometimes it may require a redesign. But the important thing is to know what is happening on the shop floor. The company must share the concerns, not only to say to someone, "Please solve it," but share the problem.' Yamamoto recalls how impressed he was on joining Toyota right out of university that 'when I made a mistake they were not angry'. It was news to British labour, too. Japanese companies were changing British attitudes toward work in corporations, as they had in the US.

Approaching every manufacturing problem from the shop

14 Toyota Crowns being loaded for delivery to the United States. The first Crowns were shipped to the USA in 1957 but sluggish sales were halted in 1960 and the Crown then redesigned for US highway use.

15 The first two Crowns exported from Yokohama to Long Beach, California in 1957 were greeted eagerly by press and public, but early models were not successful against European imports.

16 An elated Eiji Toyoda, chairman of TMC, announces the signing of the contract with General Motors on 15 February 1983 to produce vehicles jointly in California as New United Motor Manufacturing, Inc. (NUMMI).

17 Eiji Toyoda and Roger Smith, chairman of GM, riding in a Chevrolet Nova at the opening ceremony of the NUMMI joint venture.

18 Nine hundred members of the Toyota–GM joint venture, NUMMI, gather to celebrate the production of the first Chevrolet Nova in the California plant in 1984.

19 Governor Martha Layne Collins, together with Eiji Toyoda and Shoichiro Toyoda, then chairman and president of Toyota Motor Corporation, announces the agreement to site Toyota Motor Manufacturing (USA) in Kentucky in 1985

20 (Left to right) Junji Numata, General Manager, Europe Division; David Hunt, Member of Parliament, Secretary of State for Wales; Tatsuro Toyoda, Executive Vice President, Toyota Motor Company; and Barry Jones, Member of Parliament, opening a ceremonial keg of sake at the ground breaking for Toyota's UK plant in July 1990.

21 Hiroshi Okuda at the wheel of a Toyota Rav4 sport utility vehicle at an information meeting for institutional investors and analysts in London (1995).

22 Shoichiro Toyoda and his wife, Hiroko, enjoying a relaxing moment in the garden of the Kawana Hotel, on Japan's Izu peninsula during the New Year holiday, 1997.

23 Shoichiro Toyoda, chairman Toyota Motor Corporation, receives the prestigious French decoration, Commandeur de la Légion d'Honneur, from President Jacques Chirac in April, 1998.

24 President Hiroshi Okuda, left, and Chairman Shoichiro Toyoda, announce the March 1999 opening of the Toyota Mega Web auto museum, showroom and driving course in Tokyo, flanking the company's new car for Europe, the Yaris, which is marketed in Japan as Vitz.

25 A Toyota assembly worker installs a seat in a Toyota Rav4 with assistance from a specially designed robot arm at Motomachi Plant. The placards are specifications sheets called 'specifications manifest' that detail the componenets to be installed on each vehicle as it moves through final assembly.

26 Toyota's first mass-produced car, the Model AA, displayed next to the world's first mass-produced hybrid car, the Prius, in front of the headquarters building in Toyota City.

floor is basic to the Toyota system, and so is keeping records of problems, failures and problem resolution. 'I always say, let's go to the shop floor,' says Yamamoto. 'By observing the team members we get a very good opportunity to find out many things. Maybe no perfect processes exist, but we can find out many things – failures, defects, complaints or concerns of the team members – so the starting point is the shop floor. I want to establish an environment that accepts alteration. For example, if somebody is working in a posture that is not good, maybe a change in the height of the table will be beneficial. This might be a small alteration, but if it makes a worker's job easier that is good for everybody. Sometimes you see people wasting time and energy by walking too far to pick up parts, or an inspector has difficulty because of the position of the work. In those cases, change it. Sometimes a small change has a big effect.'

Yamamoto planned to work at TMUK for three years, but he has now passed five years on the job and he can see the light at the end of the tunnel. 'My challenge,' he said recently, 'is how to make this company best in terms of quality and member ownership, and maybe the target is not achieved yet. Originally the objective was to find out how to operate the company with British people. This is one of the objectives we have not reached 100 per cent, but there is now only a small gap.'

Yamamoto's British counterpart, Alan Jones, joined TMUK after more than thirty years with General Motors, and he is still intrigued and buoyed by Toyota's approach to the workforce. About two months before he got the phone calls that eventually lured him away from GM's Ellesmere Port plant in the UK, he took union representatives from his plant to the US to visit NUMMI. 'It was quite an experience,' says Jones with raised eyebrows. 'We had the reputation as one of the worst plants for labour relations in General Motors and we focused on a new – in American parlance – labour agreement which focused on relationships and flexibility. We had face to face discussions with

UAW reps, including both factions, one who supported the agreement and another not so favourably disposed.'

Jones had visited GM-affiliated plants in Japan, Isuzu and Suzuki, 'and I had an image of them, and I also had an image of NUMMI, and I went to California looking for the factors that stopped the union from feeling threatened. What stopped the union members at Fremont believing they were in between two opposing forces, union and management. I sensed that that is the worst dilemma for an employee. After all, we are all the same. Deep down we are interested not in being heroes or cowards, but going through life in a reasonable way so we can say "I got some satisfaction from what I did." The level of satisfaction for different people can be quite dramatic. Everybody wants to feel they got something out of their day. That's what I was looking for, what was it in Western culture that Toyota could do differently?'

What he discovered, he says, was a management that had analysed things 'and recognized the necessary weights to be given to various attributes. I still think that is what Toyota does remarkably well. They recognize that there are many many aspects of this business and each one deserves a consistent, appropriate weight. From time to time the focus may increase on any area, but the integrity of the base is never lost, and that is what I respect them for.'

Jones walked out of General Motors to join Toyota without a contract with the Japanese company. It did not occur to him after his interviews that he might need one. And he still doesn't have one. Recalling his hiring he says, 'I think we shook hands and I went back and told my boss and he was mesmerized by that, that after thirty years I'd walk out on GM to join a company without anything in writing. But I just knew I was going to be all right.'

STARTING FROM SCRATCH

The initial TMUK planning meetings took place in an old Derbyshire school house on makeshift desks and sample furniture. Although everyone understood that Toyota's core manufacturing principles were the key to keep in any country, there had to be local adjustment. Toyota had to fit into the local scene and be seen as a contributing member of the community, not as an outsider. Its employees would be local citizens. A smooth integration would be essential.

Said Jones, 'Frankly, people cannot work here for ten hours a day and walk out into that world out there and find it too different. They have got to be able to go home and be accepted as part of that local community. They can't be some oddity that walks around wearing a Toyota jacket. So where was the interface?' Of course that was a lot more important in the early years than now. In the early days, when Toyota was a curiosity in the little towns of South Derbyshire, says Jones, 'There were only a few of us and it was important to do things to be visible. It was necessary to go shopping in Sainsbury's wearing your jacket, to show that you are Toyota, you are not ashamed of it, but proud of it. We wanted to be clear that there was only one image of the company for everybody. That meant that status issues were key. It meant that flexibility, versatility went together, and we wanted to have a decent work ethic, an honest, hard-work ethic. I don't mean to grind anybody into the ground, but a commitment to something.' *Getting* that commitment, the Japanese coordinators told their British counterparts who would eventually run the plant, meant *giving* a commitment.

Tony Walker, general manager of the human resources division; is a transplant from Ford of Europe, where he managed several industrial relations offices. 'Not so much managing as coping, actually,' he says ruefully. He was unhappy and depressed by the confrontational labour situation at his previous jobs, and he admits the fault was not always only labour's: 'We used to have some tremendously hostile labour policies. One of the most hostile was a Dagenham policy that if the union went on strike for half a shift we laid them all off for the next half shift. We were saying to them, "If you can stop work and lose half a day's pay, so can we!"' Walker shakes his head as though in disbelief, remembering that period, in contrast to his work environment and company philosophy today: 'You cannot imagine the grind of it, and the hostility of it. Literally I had people shouting and booing and whistling as I walked down the shop floor. It is hard to understand that hostility.' (At one period hostility toward the Japanese car markers was so virulent at Ford that posters were put up in plants warning that gaps in production would be filled by 'Japs', a seriously pejorative term.) Since those days, the 1970s and 1980s, he has seen labour relations change as the Japanese car makers began moving into Britain and employing their more cooperative labour policies. But some managements remained wedded to doing things the way they were done at the home office. 'If Ford US did it,' says Walker, 'it was obviously totally the right thing to do in Europe. There was no consideration of differences of culture or distance.' He also was searching for something more precise than what he calls 'British hunch management', in which management decisions are made 'based on no data whatsoever. Where someone just says that for the next fortnight we'll do this and at the end of the fortnight we find we've wasted two weeks. I think people are much happier here at Toyota where they can understand the logic. We work hard, we work in a rational, reasoned, sensible way, with direction that is consistent and basically people think – and I am pleasantly surprised by this – think that top management know what they are doing and make the right decisions.'

This is one reason he took the job at Toyota in 1990. 'It seemed a tremendous chance to have a partnership of people working together, sharing in the same enterprise and avoiding the constant conflict. Here was Toyota, a greenfield start, no baggage. When I was approached there was no hesitation.'

Carl Klemm also leapt at the chance to join Toyota in 1990. He had been studying Toyota's methods as a production management specialist for Bedford and later for Vauxhall and had had the opportunity, after studying at the General Motors Institute in Michigan, to visit NUMMI's technical liaison office. The TLO, says Klemm, was hoping to find out what Toyota's technical secrets were, 'but it learned very quickly that a) Toyota either had no secrets, or b) that they hadn't brought them to NUMMI.

'But it did learn that the human side of Toyota was very very evident at NUMMI, in contrast to GM and therefore, although the TLO kept its name,' he says with a conspiratorial smile, 'actually it became the Toyota-Production-System-How-Do-They-Do-That? Office.'

As general manager of TMUK's car manufacturing division, Klemm has studied the Toyota system closely from inside. He finds that the primary 'engine for efficiency' is something deceptively simple: Kiichiro Toyoda's and Taiichi Ohno's insistence on minimum inventory. 'When I left GM,' he says, 'there was almost no minimum inventory policy at all. In fact it was almost "safety in inventory". The idea was to utilize each piece of equipment to its maximum. In theory the pieces and parts you were making got cheaper and cheaper because you were making more from the same investment. When I joined Toyota the first thing I noticed was the almost fanatical emphasis on minimum inventory as a driver for business efficiency. It is an extremely powerful engine,' which injects energy into the system, requiring every person to be alert and concentrated on the process.

The so-called 'soft side issues' also centred his attention immediately. 'The focus of management is on the people in two ways. One is that management shows respect for people in terms of very high expectations regardless of job title or status in the company. There is a real concern that the employee is entirely happy working here and contributing, so not only is the company receiving the maximum benefit from the employee, but the employee is receiving satisfaction from the company. You put this together with the engine of minimum inventory and it is a very powerful combination. That element that I did not see in GM was the expectation that every employee was a person on a holistic level, should contribute regardless of their job in life and their station in the company and should thereby receive some personal satisfaction from what they are doing.'

Klemm found it difficult to adjust to the Toyota way of doing things at first. He says, 'It was almost, though not quite, traumatic. A very fundamental change in my management style was necessary.' At his last job, he says, 'One needed two attributes to be a manager: strong will power, and stamina. In Toyota it required a very careful understanding of the organization and a lot of concentration on communicating.'

He learned quickly that 'whenever I met Japanese people, no matter what level, whether team leader, group leader or whatever, if I found myself operating in GM style, they would bite me, absolutely fearlessly, they would bite me and let me know "You don't treat me like that. Just tell us what you are trying to do and I will help." I had to completely change my style.

'I made many mistakes. Fortunately, under this system the workforce tell you if you are behaving badly as a manager. You get that every day in the other system – the union leaders are telling you that you are a lousy manager.'

ROSY BELLS, WORDS AND MUSIC

But as Toyota recognized different cultural traits, different local conditions, the folks sitting around the table in the schoolroom in Derbyshire had to thrash out methods of operating. They had a lot of leeway about everything except the hallowed production methods and philosophies, and the relationship between employees at different levels. The suggestion system, for example, came up for serious consideration. It has long been a fixture in Japan, where employees at many companies are still given suggestion quotas. This leads, of course, to a lot of nonsense and some good suggestions. This became a difference between Toyota Motor Corporation and some of its other plants, and TMUK. 'Each of the senior managers came from a different background,' says Klemm. 'From Ford, Rover, Vauxhall's, a big spectrum of people. What we had in common was an automotive background and we had experience with suggestion schemes in our organizations. From the beginning we had a lot of debate about the ethos of our company and what we were trying to achieve here.' When the suggestion scheme came up, 'Everybody, all around the table, from all the different companies, was frankly negative.'

What's wrong with suggestions, the Japanese coordinators wanted to know. Their managers came up with two objections. Says Klemm, 'The suggestion scheme allowed anything to be written down on a piece of paper and handed over, and some engineer or manager or somebody had to then spend time investigating whether this was a superb idea or a totally useless, harebrained, half-thought-out bit of junk that somebody had bothered to scrawl on paper. If it was a semi-good idea they had to find out how to implement it or they had to find a damn good reason why they couldn't. And then they had to explain everything to the person who'd made the suggestion, who frankly hadn't given any deep thought to the idea in the first place.' The other reason, Klemm says, was that an individual's idea was often dreamed up by someone who would keep it secret and not talk about it with their colleagues until they had submitted it. 'Then they'd talk about it and everybody else was working for this guy's benefit. A lot of other people would sweat and he would get the credit.'

The group decided they didn't want a suggestion system, which they thought could cause animosity, but what they did want was *kaizen* (improvement). 'We believed from the beginning that you are farther ahead if you take away the connection between a financial reward and the actual idea, and say, "If we all have good ideas and make progress we can have good pay rises together. After all, part of why you joined here was *kaizen*. You didn't join to put this rivet in this plate." Secondly, we recognize that nobody, or only very very few people, has an idea that comes out of their head as workable. Inventors are exceptional. We put the emphasis on recognition and we have kept it on the team level or group level, which gets rid of the negatives.'

At TMUK Klemm meets once a week with individual department managers and coordinators and the first thing on the agenda is a review of *kaizen*, which takes up the first ten minutes. Klemm explains that 'if somebody in a department has made an improvement that week it is very motivating for them that the general manager takes ten minutes to come and have a look. They feel their contribution is important, and that is the most important part of the recognition system.' There is an informal trading of *kaizen* ideas when Toyota manufacturing people visit Japan and when Japan-based members visit the overseas operations.

Alan Jones says he is constantly concerned about training and retraining team members. Newly hired team members undergo various training regimens, but after graduation some don't stick with the job despite the training exposing them to the rigours of the work. 'It's not all rosy bells,' says Jones soberly. People discover whether they are cut out to do the kind of work required of them. The biggest turnover, says Jones is in the first six or seven months 'because people have difficulty accepting that this is repetitive work. It is, and that's a fact. And we work shifts. Many people who come here may have never worked in shifts before. It looks easy, doesn't it? But it is not easy. It is hard, I think. Some people and their families can't cope with it.'

The turnover, or dropout rate, is between 7 and 10 per cent. 'We like to think we are quite good at recruiting, but obviously with this kind of turnover there are some bits missing. I think the cause is basically that you make a product every so many seconds, continually, continually, continually. People can work hard but there are always going to be some people who don't like that, and you have to respect that. I think the percentage leaving for that reason is declining because we have improved the application process.' One approach is to 'show it a little blacker' to new applicants in order to warn them just what they are getting into a bit earlier.

Tony Walker suggests that perhaps one reason for the high dropout rate – he puts it at 7–9 per cent – is that there is no assembly line work in the recruitment area and so people are not aware of the concentration required of a team member on one of the production jobs. He finds the highest dropout rate is in the early period, up to eighteen months, but after a worker has been at the job for three years he or she tends to stay.

Jones says, 'A vast majority of people come here from commercial or light manufacturing', where the pace tends to be leisurely, or at least less demanding. 'Whereas we have a line speed of say 59 seconds on one job, and 214 seconds on another. Whether you have a long work cycle or a short work cycle you have to realize that the individual worker is fully committed during that time. Unlike some other occupations, in this job he can't be doing noughts and crosses in his head at the same time. At the 214-second job he has a lot to remember, so he needs his concentration.' The longer job cycle requires the worker to do more operations or make more movements, each in a studied and practised way. 'Maybe in the short one you become conscious of the repetitions quicker. It's a factor but the degree of concentration is important.' Many people unfamiliar with modern manufacturing techniques have what Jones calls the "Charlie Chaplin image" from the movie *Modern Times*, 'where you just close your eyes and keep doing the same thing over and over. But the Toyota way doesn't allow you to close your eyes. Everything in the Toyota process is forcing everybody to be actively involved in it. You just can't throw parts at the car. You have to deal with them positively.'

The attitude of management to prospective employees is evident from the early stages. There are no 'cattle calls' in any of Toyota's recruiting; rather, it is carefully selective from the beginning, whether in Japan or abroad. Jones notes, 'You have to treat applicants with respect. Some are thinking of giving up a job they have had for years in order to come here, so you owe them that much.'

There are other reasons, of course, why people drop out. Some people sign up for a lark, find the work is difficult and decide to go back to what they were doing before, if it is available. And some are stolen away. 'We simply lose them because they have been to Toyota. It means they have more street credit. It is not a problem if they go to the local community and (our) suppliers,' says Jones, 'because in a way that is what Toyota's training is for.' Jones believes one of the responsibilities of a big company such as Toyota is to provide opportunities, to develop individuals' skills. If these people, once trained, do not fit into the Toyota system but have learned something useful that can be used elsewhere, it is a worthwhile contribution to the community. However, 'If they get targeted that's different.'

Indeed, headhunters have been having a field day at Toyota. Walker says one American car manufacturer in Britain is 'hiring Toyota people – people who have been line managers here – and putting them in consultancy or adviser roles. They are trying to change their production methods from traditional to Toyota methods, to so-called Lean Production.' Among the lures to

Toyota employees that he has heard of are overseas assignments and 'very luxurious packages'.

Sometimes there is a golden lining in the defection cloud. TMUK president Toshio Mizushima says that just after the new model Avensis was launched in 1997 the company was raided, and lost a particularly good manager. 'Everyone felt it was a big shock and would become a big problem for us. But after he left the team members, the group leaders and the senior group leaders worked very hard, and one in particular in the paint shop did such a good job that we were able to have a very successful launch without that particular manager. I told them our paint shop is the best one in the world. So it is not always bad news to have someone picked up by another company; sometimes it is a good occasion for the people.' The senior group leader was promoted to manager. 'Sometimes,' says Mizushima, 'other companies offer a double salary, a big title, a house, a car. We couldn't compete with that. But even so, we must educate our people.'

The cool Mizushima, who is now a member of the board of directors of TMC, had his baptism of labour fire before coming to TMUK. Assigned as a teacher of *kaizen* to an Australian joint venture, AMI (now AMI Toyota, Ltd) he found on his first day that there were a lot of people lounging around the office, not working. At lunchtime he went to the cafeteria and there was no one there. He soon learned that the workers walked off the job because it was too hot – 40 degrees (104 degrees Fahrenheit). 'The place was like a paint oven,' he recalls. And so in discussion with the union he worked out a rule: when the temperature hit 35 degrees (95 degrees Fahrenheit) the workers took a ten-minute break each hour. 'In other words, if it reaches 40 degrees, stop the line but don't go home. Remain and have a rest until the temperature goes down. It was one way to avoid a strike.' Dealing with peculiar non-Japanese work habits became a kind of specialty. When he tried to convince the managers at AMI to introduce the system allowing workers to stop the line, every manager refused. 'They said, if you do this, the line will never start because people will want to take a rest so they'll always pull the line-stop cord.' He hit upon a possible solution: 'I brought the managers to Japan and showed them the line and how it worked. They learned that it was very easy to find out where the problem is and where improvement is needed when you have the *andon* system. And they did it. The problem was the managers' attitude. They didn't believe in their workers. But that was an old factory and it is difficult to apply TPS to a factory with a long history.' Coming to TMUK 'was a good chance to apply my experience. It is easier to apply TPS here, but the problem is the team members do not have much experience in car manufacturing, so here we had to establish a big training centre to teach them.'

TMUK has had good labour relations, partially because of its early involvement with the five big unions that traditionally represent people in the UK car industry. 'We made presentations to them,' says senior director Bryan Jackson, 'and explained that we were going to be different. We were very open in our approach. We said we were looking for someone who wanted to work in partnership. There were two of the five that said they could work in a partnership with us, the AEU engineering union and the EETBU, the electrical workers' union. We could work with either of those, though the engineering union was closest to what we would be doing here. After we signed with the AEU they combined with the electrical union, so we got the best of both worlds. We wrote our labour agreement together and that provided the framework and showed that we were going to manage the place differently.

'I remember the president of the union went into other companies to negotiate and they said, "Why don't you give us what you gave Toyota?" and his answer was, "No problem at all. Just give *us* what Toyota gave *us*."'

Despite the huge workforce at TMUK nobody punches a timeclock. Jackson meets each new starter at the end of the week, and tells him that he can't respect or trust the worker any more than the worker can trust him. 'But I start from the point that I want to trust you and I want to respect you. I hope to earn mutual trust and respect. It is not a product of rank. I try to get the message across that it isn't just going to happen. We'll all have to work at it. The words and the music have to match. So you don't clock in. We trust you. I trust you to be here on time. I don't deduct money from you if you are a couple of minutes late. These are flags in the ground. We work hard to get these ideas across. We thought it was important to show people that we are not here to make you work to death, to make you an automaton. By having no fear or constraint on having a union, we also thought it would send a message that this is a good place where people care, and it gives them the reassurance that if something goes wrong there is a third party to come in and represent them.'

NOBODY'S PERFECT

Even an experienced person like Alan Jones, a veteran of the automobile industry, admits that after eight years at Toyota he is still trying to understand the firm and the system better. He is in good company. It is a comment frequently made by Japanese as well.

One concept he is trying to emphasize through the organization is that everyone must feel he or she is doing something worth while. 'You have got to have the opportunity to do more. Many of the people we employ here – and we do not employ right from school – get an opportunity to have another look at their life, even in a production environment.' The problem is that there is less chance of promotion because the plant has reached its 220,000-unit capacity and there is not further expansion planned which might open new avenues of advancement. 'We are looking at what we can offer these people if we can't offer straightforward organizational promotion,' says Jones. 'And we find there are a variety of things our system allows us to do very well, such as creating roles for people, treating the model cycle as an opportunity to involve people in the planning and design stages.'

He points out that all TMUK maintenance people are trained in-house and are all former production people. 'So these are like adult apprenticeships; they started three years ago.' This was part of a process of thinking ahead, envisaging that those employees who stay are probably going to stay a long time. And if that is a fact, then it becomes obvious that a change of jobs should take place over a long career. It certainly happens in the executive ranks, and also for those in other areas of the company.

'We started looking at this in a really serious way in 1994,' says Jones. 'We coined our own internal phrase, "make the job suitable for any age". Our challenge was to make the process applicable to someone for the full length of their employment here. Well, there is no Mr Average, nobody is perfect. But that is what we set up as an image. That's when we began to focus more on the mechanics of the process: how to make it so that someone could go down and do that task. Of course you have to build up the stamina. I couldn't join this company at my age and rush down to the production line. If I was thirty the question would be how to make it over the next thirty years. Can I still do the task without feeling physically shattered?'

In the old mass production system in the US and elsewhere, management grappled with the problem of middle-aged production workers who could no longer cope physically with the demands of the job. Says Jones, 'Before people got interested in TPS you could take that person and put him in the stores. This happened everywhere, in the days when everybody could sell any car they wanted.' But, he asks rhetorically, what do you do when successive employees become middle-aged? For one thing there are no more stores in TPS, no parts stockpiles to inventory and dole out. 'We can't apply that kind of solution.'

If an employee over the years loses flexibility of the joints and his muscle power is decreasing 'we should be able to design a process that doesn't require him to do all these things, like lifting seventy tons a day,' says Jones. 'This is not earth shattering; it is common sense. We have a lot of people in their thirties and a bit older. We have to bring our business in tune with the way society is going. That doesn't mean you follow the extremes, but from the beginning you can't be Toyota here and go out with your family on the weekend and be in a totally different world. They don't have to be identical, but they have to co-exist comfortably.'

He says he and his colleagues believe they are beginning to make progress on the problem: 'It starts with the interface between people and the machinery, one key part, and the other part is the team members themselves saying what is practically possible on the car. We have to get more of a discussion going with the designers in TMC. We now have to progress to the design of the car, to design it not just for manufacturing, but design for the full age spectrum, that's where we are going to go. It requires some comprehensive thinking about the tasks.' Recognition of the problems comes from the shop floor, where, for one example, the bundles of electrical wires that fan out through the car have become enormously cumbersome as accessories become more commonplace. As these wire harnesses have become bulkier they become more difficult to handle. 'You can't keep the same technology,' says Jones, 'as when we used to lay a few wires in. What are we going to do with that wire harness so that somebody can put it in, realistically? Those issues are becoming important to us.'

The problems of older employees and adjusting the workload to them are on the mind of TMC president Hiroshi Okuda. He reflected on this in an interview in Tokyo when he told me that Japan's rapidly ageing population and general demographic changes – Japan has zero population growth, and within the next couple of decades is projected to have the world's most elderly population – will bring about major changes at TMC. Engineers are revamping production lines to reduce strain, raising the work material to more comfortable heights, and creating new devices to do the heavy lifting. And it is not only older people they must cater for in Japan. Up to recently it has been impractical to have women in production jobs for a variety of reasons, not least the national law that prohibited women from working late at night. This prohibition has been dropped, and women will be welcomed on to the production line. But that means they will need labour-enhancing devices. Okuda says Toyota studies have shown that Japanese women generally have less physical strength than Western women who work in plants overseas and will need more help to cope easily with the heavier, physical side of the job. But in this and other areas, says Okuda, Toyota is looking for input from its foreign employees. He thinks they are more creative than the Japanese, and has often said so.

UK's Bryan Jackson surveys the giant Burnaston plant, now with up to 3,200 employees, and perhaps several hundred more to be hired, and ponders the question of sheer size. Considering the need for communications and personal relationships in the Toyota system, I asked, if there a limit to how large a plant can be and still retain a sense of cohesiveness and contribution?

'I think we are now facing a couple of challenges,' responded Jackson over the usual fast lunch in a cafeteria crowded with murmuring workers. 'We've got the new plant in France coming, we've got another expansion at the engine plant, we are just expanding ourselves here, and so we have a lot of new employees again. So it is almost like having to reinforce and renew the philosophy and the culture because we have hired 600 or 700 people. They are all new and there are exciting times ahead. But it is possible to get too big. Is there an outer limit? I don't know what it is. It depends on how you define the unit. Maybe a theorist would say 5,000 employees is about the right size to get the maximum benefit but I really don't have an idea. We are at 3,200 and we are going to 3,500 and I think that's OK. Obviously the thing is you do lose some opportunity. There was a time when I could walk around the assembly plant and knew everybody. Now I walk around and there are so many I don't know because I only meet them when they come in, but they know who I am. Now with the launch (of the Corolla) I spent an hour and a half with a senior group leader just going around to say hello to the guys, asking how it was going, whether they were ready. They all worked very hard, and it is an investment in saying we care, that we do understand what they are doing and how hard they have worked. I think they know that if anybody wants to stop me they can and if they ask me a question about anything. I'll answer.'

The problem that dogs Toyota plants overseas is the nagging one of compulsory overtime, which is standard at Toyota. The lighted *andon* boards in Toyota plants tell workers in decimal increments how long they will be required to work beyond their normal shift. Toward the end of 1998, as the Corolla was coming on line, TMUK was running an extra hour and a half at the end of every shift and was the only car company in the UK that was working five days and five nights. Traditionally in the UK industry people don't work Friday nights but for capacity reasons TMUK needed that extra shift's production. The solution was to schedule the Friday night shift start hours earlier than normal so workers could be finished at 3: a.m., giving them at least a small amount of sleep if they wanted to spend Saturday with their family.

Says Jones, 'Overtime is a big concern, frankly. For a short

TOYOTA

period it is OK, but we've done it for a long while. We don't want to abuse it.'

Perhaps there is one saving grace in the situation, in that overtime for one means overtime for all on board. While all manufacturing employees are working their overtime, no manager leaves before that overtime period is worked. Says Jones, 'Oh, there's always work for us to do.'

CHAPTER ELEVEN
EUROPE: STEP TWO

There was a bit of fuss at Champs Elysées no. 79 one autumn evening in 1998, as Toyota made its French début. French government officials joined Shoichiro Toyoda and other executives to inaugurate its showroom in the heart of Paris. There were smiles all around, toasts and good wishes for the venue where Toyota shows off its new creations such as the new small car, the made-for-Europe-in-Europe Yaris. In true Toyota fashion 'Le Rendez-Vous Toyota' will be used not only to encourage visitors to see their Toyota dealers, but also to tell them about what Toyota is up to in the areas of environmental action and new technology. It can display four vehicles or so, and offers big screen displays, computers to use, stacks of information and a tea lounge called the Cyber-café. But you can't buy a Toyota at Le Rendez-Vous; you can just look and perhaps be impressed and maybe even intrigued enough to want to take a test-drive. It is not really about selling; there are other outlets for that. It is about identity, which the company lacks in Europe despite sales of more than half a million cars a year. Toyota hopes to use the facility to hold non-commercial cultural events as well, as part of Toyota's belated attempt to become a major industrial player on the Continent.

Nearly a decade ago Shoichiro Toyoda said he recognized that some prize markets were going unexploited and that, while Toyota was basking in the good times, it had become 'a bit self-satisfied, perhaps arrogant'. It was then, as the 1990s approached, that plans for an outreach to the world's second biggest car market, Europe, really took shape. With the construction of production facilities in Britain, a design studio and new parts distribution centre in Belgium and plans for full-scale production in France, Toyota was on the way to tapping the European market, hopefully big time. Europe has been a virtual cash cow for America's Big Three for many years, and although Toyota had not totally neglected the European market there was room for improvement.

In the early 1980s Toyota did quite well, selling as many as 300,000 cars a year in Europe. But by the mid-1980s the flood of Japanese exports became headline news in Europe, and quotas on many things Japanese were imposed. There were two kinds of restrictions: those of the European Union or the European Commission; and then the national restrictions applied by such countries as France, Italy, Spain, Portugal and the UK. What the Europeans complained about was their lack of access to the Japanese market, and in retaliation they curbed Japanese imports. Italy, for example, was so restrictive that it virtually demanded car for car sales reciprocity. But what the restrictions said mutely was that local production was the only sure way of being a big player in the markets, if you could get in.

Tatsuo Takahashi is president and CEO of Toyota Motor Europe Marketing & Engineering (TMME), a company set up in Belgium to oversee and coordinate Toyota sales and parts distribution as well as product planning activities. A veteran of overseas ventures, he says Toyota until recently has been doing its European business 'by remote control' but it was evident for some time that it would become important to be on the local scene. The UK plant was the first step, but full continental production was the next logical move. He says it is likely that in a stable European market, with little growth, his company is going to have to 'seize market share' from the other car makers.

The first UK-built car, the Carina E, came off the line at Burnaston in December, 1992, and much of the plant's production of its successors, the Avensis and the Corolla, since then has gone to the Continent. Beyond the problem of its own historical conservatism or financial self-satisfaction, Toyota's problem in raising sales volume in Europe was complicated by an expensive yen, tariffs, national restrictions, quotas and other factors, most of which are dropping away with the arrival of true European unification. And some say the less than exciting design of Toyota offerings, despite their reputation for quality, has held the company back until now. The acceptance of Burnaston's 80 per cent local content cars as European was a major step, and Toyota is counting on the addition of its new plant at Valenciennes in northern France, another full-fledged European car operation, to make it a major player in the market.

That is not to say that Toyota has a free ride in Europe, even with two assembly plants there. While the quotas are scheduled to drop away by the year 2000, the French have attempted to extend the system or amend it in such a way as to keep a kind of oversight on the foreigners. Some French motor industry voices have complained that, with overcapacity in their industry estimated at as much as 20 per cent, Toyota's entry with a plant in France will only exacerbate the problem, and that Toyota's jobs at the new plant will only take workers away from other local companies. Actually, unemployment in Nord prefecture where the new plant is to be built has been as high as 20 per cent, and the French government has been encouraging to Toyota.

PASSIONATE ABOUT CARS

It is a fact of life that much emotion has arisen in Europe about cars. Car companies are expressions of patriotism, especially in Germany, France, Italy and Sweden. One could argue that taxpayer aid to car companies in trouble in these countries has contributed to the overcapacity problem. Industry officials in the US have said that if companies were allowed to fail there would naturally be no overcapacity. Company bailouts of one kind or another take place, as they did with Chrysler in the US, with Renault in France and with Fiat in Italy as a matter of national pride, political expediency, a way of providing continuing employment, all in one way or another understandable, even laudable, goals.

A Toyota official in Belgium puts the situation in a nutshell when he says governments are very touchy about what happens in the car industry and that 'if you handle it badly you can get in a lot of trouble'. The closing of a Renault plant in Belgium in 1997 became a national scandal because of the abrupt way it was done, with what was considered insufficient notice, which made it an issue in the European Commission and the European Parliament. The newspapers and television stations had a field day with the story. Because of the very size of the car industry and nature of the business a wide spectrum of the population gets involved – governments, unions, consumers, environmentalists, bankers, lawyers, even people who can't afford cars.

Nevertheless, auto company officials think the game is worth the candle. And on the cusp of the new millennium Toyota is making a major play with a new organization, a new plant, and a new entry level car as the cutting edge of its strategy. To push ahead aggressively Toyota hired the dynamic and articulate Juan Jose Diaz Ruiz as sales chief for Europe. Diaz Ruiz was in charge of worldwide sales and marketing for Volkswagen AG's Audi division, and he comes to Toyota with a mission, in his own words, 'To make Toyota a fully integrated player in the European market.'

Long intrigued by Toyota's vacillation over Europe, Diaz Ruiz says that as a professional in the industry 'you are always watching "the machine that changed the world"'. He got to know Toyota through the VW–Audi connection with Toyota in Japan, which provides cars for sale through Toyota outlets.

When he was approached to join Toyota in 1997, he was intrigued because he had long wondered when Toyota would make a move on Europe and why it allowed other Japanese companies to get a foothold there first. He says he took the job 'with alacrity'.

'I was always fascinated by the fact that Toyota was so weak in Europe, had no face in Europe, no apparent strategy in Europe and no apparent philosophy to go about conquesting the second largest market in the world. (Author's note to the reader unaccustomed to arcane motor industry sales jargon: selling your brand of car to a person who had previously bought somebody else's brand is called conquesting, from the manufactured verb 'to conquest'.)

'Now (by taking the job) perhaps I could answer the question I had been asking myself for the last ten years,' he says. 'Why had Toyota neglected Europe?' Diaz Ruiz learned the car business at Ford of Europe ('some say it is the best business school in the world'), where he became vice-president for sales and marketing in Spain. The Spanish joint venture SEAT, which was affiliated with Fiat of Italy, was devastated when in 1982 Fiat decided to pull out. 'It was trauma for Spain,' recalls Diaz Ruiz. There were 30,000 families without a job and it affected another 35,000 indirectly. 'SEAT started looking for partners. They were talking to Toyota and at that time Toyota was obviously already thinking, one way or another, of moving into Europe.' For whatever reasons, SEAT became more attractive to VW and it became part of the VW group. Diaz Ruiz arrived at SEAT a month after talks with Toyota ended. 'I kept asking myself, if in 1982 Toyota was thinking of Europe, why didn't they make another move until 1997?' he says. 'Why sixteen years in the meantime? Honda had increased capacity in Europe, producing more than 400,000 units, and the company that had the power, the know-how, the quality and the image did nothing.'

He suggests that there has been a change in management style due to Hiroshi Okuda. 'He has changed the mentality of the Toyota people. Today I do not find Toyota much more conservative than any of the other companies I have worked for. I have worked for many people who are now running Ford and until recently Chrysler, and I must say that I don't feel that Toyota is a very conservative company.'

To illustrate he says that when he came to Toyota he looked over the model line-up and at one particular car, and 'I thought, Omigod, this is a real weakness.' As luck would have it, two weeks later Okuda and Akihiro Wada, an engineer who is executive vice-president for product development, came to visit and Diaz Ruiz expressed his concern about the marketability of the car. A week later, on his first official trip to Japan, he met the chief engineer of the car and 'to my great surprise, within two months it was decided to make a major change'. The plan was for a major facelift in eighteen months, 'and I could see the prototype within two months'.

'No manufacturer I know would have been more dynamic or more responsive to a market need. This required a substantial investment, too. In this business it is extremely important to be rational, professional and to be able to combine the human capacity to communicate with very hard facts that appeal to business common sense. Once these factors are put together, this company reacts like no other company I know, and I have worked for Audi, VW, Ford, SEAT, and now Toyota. I think president Okuda is responsible, for having this capacity to say, "Gentlemen, if we see there is a problem we have to react. The worst thing you can do is waste time when the information is so obvious and so clear."'

LOOMING CHALLENGES

Still, no one denies that Toyota faces real challenges in Europe as the new player on the ground. Diaz Ruiz sees the company's requirements as manifold: 'We need a new image, a comprehensive strategy, a stronger dealer organization, and systems to cope with one market, one price, one currency, one everything,' as European unity becomes a fiscal reality. Over lunch in the understated elegance of the Brussels headquarters, Diaz Ruiz says his programme, called Challenge 2000, designed to set Toyota on a strong foundation in the twenty-first century, coincides with 'the biggest challenge Europe has faced since the beginning of the last century'. His plan, which was approved in two months, provided for a major change of the European organization, employing new people, splitting the organization by brand – a Toyota brand director and a Lexus brand director, a new market development director, and changes in communications and other systems. 'In four months,' he says, gesturing, 'we have changed the face of the company completely.'

Okuda told his staff to remember that Europe is different, not to treat it as an extension of the United States. Diaz Ruiz points out that Europe is a continent where the people speak thirteen major languages 'and where we have so many nationalities, cultures and so on, that this complexity requires a different approach. We are a similar/different region. There are a lot of things that unite us and a lot of things that divide us. The key issue for a business strategy is to identify the things that are common.' It sounds like the 'Think Global, Act Local' refrain heard so often now among multinationals.

'Europeans are always looking to be different. We are probably the most creative and anarchic people in the world. Everybody is fighting to be different, to express himself in what they do, what they consume, what they drive, how they dress, where they go. This is so important to the European, while in other places people are fighting to conform. Europe is about your individuality.'

The complexity for a manufacturer becomes obvious quickly. As Diaz Ruiz puts it, 'A car has to meet basic needs like safety, protection to the environment, it must be pleasing to the eye –

these needs are global, minimum standards. In southern Europe air conditioning is almost basic; in Scandinavia it's nice to have. A strong heating system is a must in Scandinavia; in the south it's nice to have. Heated seats in the north or in Germany are fantastic, especially when you are out of your car for three hours and you come back and your car is covered with snow. But I come from the south of Spain, from Cordoba, where in the shadow you are likely to get 43 degrees (109°F). A heated seat in Cordoba is like you are offending people. All of this means that you have to have a modular system. We have to be able to admit variation.'

In a very real way the New Europe, if it comes about as completely as many hope, will make it easier for all car makers to sell, despite regional desires for special features. But those features will be no less important. (Nobody expects automatic transmissions, for example, to become as popular in Europe as they are in the United States. In northern Europe only 15 per cent of cars are sold with automatic transmission, in southern Europe a mere 3 per cent.)

'In the old days,' he says, 'we used to have each country with its own individual model type. Today that is gone and we have one type of car all over Europe, and very soon we will have a Europe with one price.' That price information will also be available to everyone on the internet, which is also likely to have an impact on the way cars are sold. In the United States today more than 15 per cent of car shoppers say they have done some investigation on the internet, and the number is climbing.

A major problem for Toyota in the European environment is that Europeans are image driven, with car makes that are national symbols, national champions. One could call it chauvinism, xenophobia or just national pride, but the preference for a national car, or a car with the comfortable old symbol, such as the Mercedes-Benz three-pointed star, is a factor. Brand names are big in Europe, as they are in Japan. But Toyota does not yet have the kind of 'face' that marketers say it needs. As one American analyst puts it, 'Toyota has always had a problem putting character into their cars'.

'That is one of our big jobs here in Europe,' says TMME's James Rosenstein, who heads the communications group. And it comes from a lot of misinformation about Japan and the Japanese that has never been corrected and the Japanese have never worked very hard to correct. The fact that Europeans cannot put a 'face' to things Japanese 'largely comes from ignorance and prejudice,' posits Rosenstein, and it affects the way they think about Japanese cars. 'People in Europe often think of the Japanese as the faceless hordes of Asia. They still fear that the robots from Japan are going to come and take us over. You still see stories about Japanese going to work at six a.m. and doing callisthenics and singing the company song before work.'

Building a bright identity is one of the challenges Diaz Ruiz was brought in to tackle. He is trying to create 'brands within a brand' because Toyota is not content to sell a model or two, since it has a range of cars to sell. It has models not yet sold in Europe that could be adapted for the market. 'We want Toyota to cover every sector of the market,' says Diaz Ruiz. 'The problem is that in every segment you need a very different marketing strategy, a different approach to the customers. You need different organizations because some customers with an entry model like the Yaris are prepared to accept a level of service and customer attention that somebody in a Land Cruiser or a Lexus is not.'

The plan is to set up four vehicle lines, or four lines of business:

The Comfort and Enjoyment business, or the core business, will handle standard and traditional values of transportation with style and roominess, with Yaris, Avensis, Corolla and Camry models. This segment will be about 70 per cent of the business, Diaz Ruiz estimates.

The Leisure and Fun business will sell trendy and sporty

models, coupés, cabriolets, and off-road vehicles, together with family vehicles such as minivans.

The Executive segment, for the Lexus range which will be sold at separate franchises, will include the current line plus a new model, the IS200 sedan.

The Business segment is for commercial vehicles. This may also include small vans.

Diaz Ruiz says in future cars will be developed for the specific lines, and the lines will develop the ways they market the vehicles. The target is to boost sales to 600,000 in the year 2000. It will mean adding about five hundred dealers to its network, mainly in southern Europe, where restrictions have been the heaviest, bringing the total to about 2,800 by 2005, not including the new Lexus franchises. The rationale for this is that 'a new level of specialization will enable us to take care of these customers as individuals. Now we are treating them all the same, whether somebody has spent DM50,000 for a Camry or DM14,000 for a Yaris, yet they are two different types of customers. You cannot treat them the same.'

This is the strategy, at least as it is being formulated. 'It is the only way to compete with our European competitors,' Diaz Ruiz insists. 'Toyota is a company that is quick to react when there is a clear plan and a clear direction in which to go. I think they understand in Toyota City that Europe is a very complex market. I think the issue was probably to take the decision to incorporate a given number of Europeans and give them the trust to get on with the job. I can imagine the problem for my [Japanese] colleagues to come here from a country where there is enormous pressure to conform, and enter this *terra incognita*. It was the brave decision to say, "OK, if we want to succeed in Europe we have to do it the way the Europeans do it."'

AND BEYOND

The European market, of course, is more than just the affluent West, and Toyota has set its sights on all of it. Before Russia's economic collapse the company opened a representative office there; it was planned to build vans there from imported kits, to start up the business, though Okuda says plans for Russian production are now on hold. But in 1997, in a small training room in Moscow with one instructor, 180 Russians took an automotive course. In 1997, Toyota sold 10,000 vans in Russia. Poland (9,300 units) and the Czech Republic and Slovakia (4,300 units) have small Toyota operations and the company is keeping its options open for the future all through the former Eastern bloc.

Akira Yokoi, an executive vice-president for international operations, says, 'Russia has a potential; it used to be a two million vehicle market, and I think there is a high probability that this will be revived one day. But Russia is still uncharted for us, and that is why we opened a new representative office in Moscow. It is just the first step toward the future.'

Yokoi, an easy-smiling man with a mop of salt-and-pepper hair, says the general company vision is to produce six million vehicles soon after the turn of the century, of which 2.5 million will be built overseas. 'The dream is not unrealistic,' he says. 'Last year we built a total of 4.8 million, and we now have production bases all over the world.' His view of what is realistic is based on known factors, but there are a lot of unknowns. 'We hope to be one of the pillars of the world's Big Three, but that is just a vision. Before we get to that we have to face lots of issues.' First is to have the right product for each market and secondly, he says, Toyota has to be able to respond to world requirements in terms of environmental protection and conservation of resources, making the company and its products welcome in the markets where it sells. And/or wishes to produce vehicles.

The most pressing requirement to fulfil the grandiose vision Toyota has for itself is the staff to do the job. Says Yokoi, 'We especially need to procure and nurture personnel with wisdom. We need people of quality, not in a very abstract way, but people who can be instrumental in the work we must achieve. We have not found enough of them yet. If we are not able to do this we cannot achieve true globalization.' The company is planning to launch 'Toyota Universities' in Europe and the US, which would consist of lecture series at selected universities designed to develop recruits to take responsible positions in the international company. The courses would be given over a period of three to five years.

'I'm telling all my staff members we have finished the era of working in one single country,' says Yokoi. 'So I might ask my American staff to work in Europe, or the Australians to work in Asia. This is how we can make effective use of Toyota's resources. Since these will be global positions our young Japanese will not be able to be lazy because of all the competition.'

Many of Japan's senior executives, Yokoi included, got their experience by being tossed into international situations where they were actually out of their depth. We have met some earlier in this publication. Yokoi was sent to Thailand when he was twenty-eight and relatively new to the company. Even at that young age he had as many as seventy people working for him. 'I was lucky,' he says, 'that I learned to manage such a staff. They were all Thai people and had a totally different background from mine, and I had to put the team together toward one single goal. This was precious experience. It was on-the-job training for me. They [the Toyota management] wanted to throw me into the experience and measure me according to Toyota criteria.' Among the things he learned was the importance of constant commun-ication. Then, in ten years in Indonesia, he learned how to deal with powerful governments and an unstable social situation under Sukarno and later Suharto. 'In an unstable country,' he says, 'I learned that it is not enough to bring your company together. I had to plug into the network everywhere – the army, the student movement, the government, the ministry of finance, the ministry of industry, and so on.' Like a good diplomat, Yokoi learned to represent his company with fairness and dignity and get along with the government. The pay-off came years later: in the revolution in 1998, when rampaging Indonesians destroyed many properties, the Toyota production facilities which produce the Kijang vehicle were not damaged. 'We have to give ourselves credit,' he says with a smile, 'that if I look around the world in the past ten years or so we have had no damage to our facilities. I think we are doing the appropriate things in each place.'

Whether today's young Japanese are prepared and able to do what their predecessors have done, or will be given the chance, is an open question. Yokoi points out that today Toyota has a lot of facilities worldwide, 'so that if a person is really ambitious and wants to achieve something, things that used to take twenty years to accomplish they will now be able to do in ten years'. It all depends, he suggests, on the psychology of the individual: 'Whether they have the hungry spirit that we had is another story.' (There is also a still-open question as to just how far a non-Japanese will be able to go in the organizational structure, even with the necessary drive and fluency in the Japanese language.)

The company was very different in 1962, when a sense of patriotism, of pride in national development, imbued Japan's eager and hard-working workforce as the country was finally emerging from the shadow of its militarist past and abject defeat. 'My only motive in joining Toyota was that I wanted to contribute to the Japanese economy by getting what the economy most needed: dollars. And so working overseas I was able to do this,' he says. 'We had this big national target to achieve. Now the

greatest challenge in affluent Japan is to see if people can make
their own personal achievement. In our era things were simple.
Our task now is to stimulate the young people to feel this hunger.'
It may be the hardest job he has been handed so far.

CHAPTER TWELVE
THE GREENER ROAD AHEAD

The snub-nosed Prius responded instantly to my foot on the accelerator, startling me just a bit. There was no sound – well, perhaps a bit of a whine or whirr, but it was indistinct. As I pulled away from Toyota headquarters and into traffic, a gentle computerized female voice purred that I should make a left turn at the first intersection and informed me that it was 100 metres ahead. I saw the intersection both through the windscreen and on the electronic navigational system map display on the dashboard. The man in the passenger seat beside me pushed a button and the screen switched to an active schematic diagram of the drive system of this, the world's first mass production hybrid car. Moving arrows showed how the power was flowing, first from battery power. Now, with increased speed, the gasoline engine had started silently and was powering the car. Without the vivid display I would not have known when it happened in the car's innards. This smooth transition from battery power to engine power, to a combination and back to battery seemed a silent marvel to me, if not to my companion, the chief engineer of the Prius project, Takeshi Uchiyamada. The Prius, on sale in Japan since 1997, is major evidence, if any were needed, that Toyota is taking the challenge of the environmental age seriously. For this machine is said to improve fuel economy by at least 100 per cent, to emit 90 per cent less pollution under Japanese city driving conditions (when compared to current Japanese regulations), and its nickel-metal hydride batteries never need external charging, since the engine and the braking system keep the batteries charged. The Prius is being prepared for the different driving conditions it will have to face in Europe, the US and elsewhere.

Toyota claims it gets twice the fuel economy of a similar car powered by a conventional gasoline engine only, which also means it will also emit correspondingly less carbon dioxide and other pollutants. Akihiro Wada, Toyota's executive vice-president for product development, says some owners of Priuses are claiming a 100 per cent increase in gasoline mileage.

The spare, athletic Uchiyamada smiles at the notion because, when he was given the assignment to build an altogether new car, his plan was to improve fuel efficiency to 150 per cent of that of existing cars. The response from top management was surprising. 'They said that the 150 per cent target is not good enough for the car of the twenty-first century. The only way I could see to achieve a 200 per cent target was to use the hybrid system. Now that I look back, I think the high target and the big challenge was the driving force for us to accomplish this.'

Setting targets is a way of life at Toyota and, though some employees may not appreciate the constant exhortations to these goals, there is no gainsaying the importance of the goals chosen. The impact on the environment of the cars Toyota builds and sells is a matter of great concern and management is trying to get everyone in the company to understand that their future depends on making that impact smooth and even beneficial.

Around Toyota offices and factories employees sport a little green lapel pin in the shape of a car but with a tracing of the veins of a leaf running through it. It is a reminder of the commitment to environmental leadership that Hiroshi Okuda and the board of Toyota have made for themselves and their company. The move toward 'greener' cars means a reduction in the use of fossil fuels and the emission of noxious pollutants, cleaner production plants and processes, and vehicles that are more readily recyclable when they are no longer serviceable. The search for ways to meet the demands of what Okuda calls the new business model for the twenty-first century is exhaustive, and not yet altogether successful, but the challenge is nevertheless being tackled from several angles.

Okuda says that, despite its considerable efforts so far, Toyota will have to increase its research and development budget beyond its current 6 per cent of sales. 'American auto companies such as GM and Ford are spending about 8–9 per cent,' he says. 'Even if compared by total amounts, these companies are spending more than us.' Despite that, he insists that 'generally speaking, in terms of technology those who are ahead are said to be Mercedes in Europe and, in Japan, Toyota'.

The technology goals Toyota is pursuing include newer kinds of internal combustion engines, electric vehicles of various kinds, cleaner factories, better recycling, and an 'intelligent transport system' (ITS) that embraces these technologies and bundles them with new information and communications capabilities. The ITS treats automobiles not as discrete entities but as components in an overall system that includes the streets and highways as well as the urban infrastructure. A joint study team sponsored by business, government and academia in Japan called the Vehicle, Road, Traffic Intelligence Society (VERTIS) estimates that intelligent transport systems could reduce traffic congestion by 50 per cent over ten years and 80 per cent in twenty years. There would be very large reductions in pollutants as a result. Shoichiro Toyoda is chairman of the nationwide organization, and Okuda is chairman of an organization working on the automated highway system.

Toyota's conceptual contributions include, for example, a dual-mode bus powered by a battery-driven motor and a thrifty but conventional engine that picks up passengers normally, then enters a special guideway and is automatically whisked along at 95 miles an hour on its electric motor, leaving the guideway to deliver its passengers normally. The system is in the experimental prototype stage. Automated driving lanes for private cars or trucks would provide a way for tired drivers to get safely to their destinations.

Toyota's Highway Traffic Information System is also in developmental use. The system employs a small video screen on the dashboard that shows a real time view of the traffic conditions at a selected crucial junction on the road ahead, helping the driver to make decisions on the route he wishes to take. The idea is to allow drivers to avoid choke points so that traffic systems can flow in a smoother stream. The Highway Traffic Information System uses FM transmissions and fibre optical networks to deliver this information, and is already in use in Tokyo and Osaka. A system used during the 1998 winter Olympic Games in Nagano, Japan, offered drivers information on traffic conditions and alternate route suggestions and approximate timings to the competition venues.

In some cities the traffic delays at toll booths on bridges, expressways and at tunnels can be alleviated by an electronic identification system that automatically bills the user as the vehicle breezes past the sensor without delay. Other ideas being developed: How about entering a parking lot or garage and having your onboard navigation system direct you to an open parking space? Or sensors embedded in highways to relay information on road or traffic conditions? Or radar cruise control that senses the traffic and regulates car speed to avoid collisions, and can sense a slower moving car ahead and safely overtake it automatically? (A demonstration car has been shown in the US.)

Toyota is also using the global positioning satellite network in its navigational system, which it calls the Dynamic Route Guidance System, now very popular in Japan. The global positioning satellite network is operated by the US Defense Department and it sends a somewhat degraded signal to civilian users, which does not allow for pinpoint accuracy. Toyota technicians have developed a system that takes the GPS result and corrects the error before relaying it to the vehicle system. The Monet (mobile network) will provide a wide array of information to a motorist on request, including traffic and road information, location of facilities, the movie schedule (you can buy a ticket from your car) and news. You can also pick up your e-mail.

Executive vice-president Kosuke Yamamoto points out that 'we are still at the experimental stage of these technologies', and notes pointedly that 'of course the core business of Toyota is the automobile. But when we think about the future, there is an absolute need to cultivate new business. In addition, in order to overcome the so-called hollowing out of Japanese industry it is necessary to develop new technologies.'

CONSERVING AND BUILDING

In a well-kept forest preserve not far from Toyota headquarters at Toyota City, researchers are blending technologies to learn more about how trees and plants clean the atmosphere and how reforestation can be employed and accelerated. Toyota's central R&D labs are also studying pollutants such as nitrous oxides, carbon dioxide, ozone, suspended particulate matter such as smoke from diesel engines and acid rain, and their biological effects.

In the auto building world, the company is attempting to make its environmental efforts known and to encourage outside citizen participation as well as that of its team members. At Toyota's Kentucky assembly plant, for example, students from Scott County High School have been invited routinely, as part of a school programme, to take water samples from creeks and streams around the plant to test for any damaging discharges. The Kentucky plant also accepts hazardous waste from citizens for safe disposal – in 1997 as much as 280,000 pounds was collected. At NUMMI in Fremont, California, a committee of team members recommended ways to conserve water and recycle, cutting total usage by 320,000 gallons a day. Paint sludge is being turned into landscaping bricks. When the giant presses stamp out car doors, the squares of steel from the cut out window area are shipped to suppliers of smaller parts for their use. Other cut steel is compressed into 350-pound cubes and sent back to the steel mill to be remade into sheet steel, thereby sparing the landfills. Of course almost all of the parts-carrying *kanban* crates and boxes are collapsible and reused constantly for about four years, and then recycled to make new ones.

But the bottom line is the car itself. And that's where the R&D budgets eat up the money Okuda was talking about. Toyota has a 12,000-member R&D team working toward the ultimate ecologically clean cars, attempting to clear the technological obstacles in their way.

Electric cars are fine but the batteries are heavy, need to be recharged frequently and have a short range. Diesel engines are smoky and noisy and accelerate poorly. Conventional gasoline engines work well but even the best emit pollutants. Hybrid cars, which use both a conventional engine and a battery-driven electric motor, are an interim solution positioned between the current gasoline engine cars and the ideal electric car powered by a fuel cell. The fuel cell, a device that uses a neutral fuel such as hydrogen, generates electricity without combustion and gives off only heat and water vapour as by-products. But the fuel cell is conceded to be many years away from practical and economical use. Akihiro Wada says that while a lot of progress has been made on the development of this alternative power source, internal combustion engines as we know them will power the majority of vehicles on the road for decades in the future. 'People often say that the electric vehicle age will come very soon,' Wada says. 'However, if that age ever comes then we must have a very big breakthrough.'

Like many others in the industry Wada sees a constant updating of our conventional vehicles as the most logical. For one thing, the research is expensive and time-consuming. For another, consumer costs would be high. Electric vehicles are now extremely expensive to produce and so far have been put on the market at a loss to the maker. One analyst in Japan estimates that for Toyota to make money on its Prius it will have to ramp up production (and sales) thirteen times. General Motors does not even sell its smart little EV-1; rather, it leases the machine, and there has been no great clamour to sign up. The batteries to power automobiles are expensive, and Wada points out that, if you need to replace a dead battery system during the lifetime of your car, 'The cheapest battery would be about the same price as what you paid for the vehicle. We need inexpensive and long-lasting batteries to have a viable system.' Also, he says, 'It is not so beautiful for the environment' because of the need to recharge electric vehicle batteries with energy generated some-where else, usually with fossil fuels, and then there is the problem of proper disposal of hazardous battery material. Okuda's view of the search for the Zero Emissions Vehicle is that the goal is worth striving for despite the cost. He says the aim of Toyota is to produce fuel cell cars prior to Mercedes. Mercedes has announced it will do so by the year 2004. But the cost of fully electric vehicles is not inconsiderable. He estimates that the cost per unit of a fully electric vehicle would be about $85,000 and the most you could expect people to pay for them is about half of that. In the meantime, Toyota is making progress with battery power. Its RAV4 EV is an SUV that the company claims can reach speeds of 125 kilometers an hour and can travel 200 kilometers on a charge.

Wada points out that the desire of consumers for cars still largely hinges on the availability and price of fuel. When and if fuel supplies dwindle and fuel cells are in demand, there will still be another problem, says Wada. You have to give the fuel cell some fuel in order for it to generate electricity. 'The difficulty here is what will be the fuel for the fuel cells. In the US gasoline and methanol are the candidates. Hydrogen is very simple but, if you think of the infrastructure, then hydrogen is difficult to use on the market.' Methanol, alcohol and natural gas have also been tried as fuel cell fuels. Beyond that, so far, fuel cells developed by Toyota and other companies in Europe and Canada do not yet give out much power. With a fuel cell the size of the engine compartment, says Wada, the speed achievable now is low: 'The vehicle could participate in a parade, that's all.'

Realistically, Wada says, 'We need to develop new engines and systems like the hybrid, and if the price of fuel increases in the future then consumers will buy fuel efficient cars even if the price is high.' Toyota has demonstrated an experimental fuel cell-powered RAV4 using Toyota's own fuel cell fuel system, which consists of a heavy metal alloy that absorbs and holds large amounts of hydrogen, but the question of what fuels to use eventually to power fuel cells has not been answered. Daimler-Chrysler, Ford and a company called Ballard Power Systems have teamed up to produce fuel cells to power automobiles, trucks and buses, and Ballard claims its cells will eventually meet performance and range requirements for autos, buses and trucks. Other Japanese companies such as Nissan and Honda, and Sweden's Volvo and Germany's Volkswagen are also using Ballard fuel cells in their experiments. Toyota will develop its own, as it prefers.

Toyota's newly designed small turbo-charged diesel engine with direct injection and other innovations is said to be quiet, smooth, cleaner and with better acceleration capability than conventional diesels. It will be installed in cars built in Europe, where diesel engines are popular. Toyota's D-4 gasoline engine claims 30 per cent better mileage, lower emissions and a 10 per cent increase in power due to its extremely lean gas/air mixture, which is injected around the spark plugs instead of filling the intake ports with a richer mixture. A new type of catalytic converter is used with the D-4 engine. Research on making the engine even cleaner is continuing even as the engine is being installed in vehicles in Japan. There is also ongoing research on powering engines with compressed natural gas and other fuels.

If fuel savings and low emissions are a goal, many feel that the simplest way to this end is by reducing the weight of the vehicle. By cutting the weight of a car dramatically the amount of engine power needed, hence the size of the engine, could be correspondingly reduced. Theoretically, with enough weight reduction a car accustomed to a six-cylinder power plant might be able to provide acceptable performance with a four- or even three-cylinder engine.

THE FIRST HYBRID CAR

Making products people want while fulfilling the demands of environmentally sound practice may seem like a difficult task. 'We feel it is our mission to develop new vehicles that consumers would want to purchase, or replace their old vehicle with,' says Okuda. 'We want to introduce attractive products.' That doesn't mean, he adds, that they will not be environmentally friendly. Okuda is on the record as saying that 'we at Toyota do not believe environmental protection and economic growth are mutually exclusive . . . if people in the twenty-first century continue to choose automobiles as their primary method of transportation our industry must lead the way toward new social standards. I am convinced that the automotive industry must practise sustainable development and set the pace in developing solutions that protect our environment.'

When Takeshi Uchiyamada was given the charter to develop the car that became the Prius he was given no strait-jacket, but an open charter under Toyota's chief engineer system. A chief engineer put in charge of a project has equal or higher rank than the various department heads whose engineers, designers and technicians will work on aspects of his project, thereby obviating many potential roadblocks due to power struggles and the like.

It is a system that goes back to the post-war era when chief engineers from Japanese aircraft companies came into Toyota. In the aircraft industry such single person coordination was normal and, when the war was over, many engineers were out of work as all the aircraft plants that had not been destroyed were shut down. Early Toyota cars were made lighter by these aircraft engineers, who were always conscious of weight saving. Some of these engineers were responsible for development of Japan's famed Bullet Train, whose wagons and power units were constructed along aircraft lines.

Uchiyamada is too young to have learned to be a chief engineer in the Second World War. He came directly to Toyota from the University of Nagoya in 1969 and was put in charge of improving the noise and vibration of Toyota's front drive cars. His team developed the isolated anti-vibration sub-frame for the Lexus ES300 and was recognized for triumphs in the area of smooth running and low noise cars.

'Prius was a project assigned from the top,' he says, 'with a directive to make a car for the twenty-first century. It was a very vague directive so I had to start by coming up with the concept.' He set two goals. One was to maintain the current practicability of the car that people now enjoy. The second, he says, was 'to face the many issues cars of the future will be facing'. That meant the car's relationship to the use of resources, and the environment. 'So I started to develop a car which is fun and convenient to drive and at the same time environmentally friendly.

'There was one big challenge to overcome in developing the car,' continues Uchiyamada. 'We were told that there is no need to use conventional parts. Now it is our custom to try to utilize parts from existing models in developing the next generation model. It cuts down costs. However, with the Prius we were free to try completely new things. But this turned out to be more of a burden for us because we were allowed to design new parts from scratch, but it meant that whenever we did something we had to ask ourselves why, and the answer had to be acceptable.'

How to start, then? From the inside out. 'What we did was to try to forget totally about existing cars and to figure out what is the best position for a person to be seated in a certain space. We had to forget about the platform, the engine and the suspension. We first tried to find the best height for the hip point in order to make it easy to get in and out. And once we had the height of the hip point and the positioning of the buttocks, then we worked out what is the best position, the most comfortable posture for a person to sit. That way, once we had the best position for one person in a certain space we can see what kind of space is needed for other people, and subsequently determined the best positioning for four adults in the car.

'Up to then we had just space and people. But we had no car. It was only after we had the positioning for four people to sit that we could think about the hardware. After we fixed the cabin we tried to design the external shape of the car.' The actual planning of the suspension and the platform on which to build the car would be brand new, as he had been allowed. This in itself was quite a concession, considering how customary it is to use existing parts and platforms in the interest of economy. Taking unnecessary parts out and designing simpler parts to put in has been one route to weight- and money-saving at Toyota. Relying on proven technology does not necessarily mean a cheapening or compromising of the product. For example, Takeshi Yoshida, chief engineer for the Corolla at Toyota's Vehicle Development Center II, points out that his car is assembled in 15 countries, and sold in 150 nations in 52 different body styles, but all are built on the same platform, from hatchback to minicar to coupé. Yoshida boasts that the popular Corolla has the biggest volume base in the world, with more than one million built as of 1997, and is still going strong.

Uchiyamada's challenge, of course, was to get high fuel efficiency but the initial assignment did not necessarily require a hybrid engine, although the concept had been around at least since Ferdinand Porsche took part in a car rally with a hybrid car back in 1905. Detroit has experimented for many years with the idea and with other ways of conserving fuel. I once drove an experimental car in Detroit that had an eight-cylinder engine that could be switched to operate on only four cylinders at the driver's option. The idea never got near production.

'There were several technical problems to be solved before commercialization of the hybrid engine,' says Uchiyamada, with understatement. 'Among them were two major issues. One was the battery problem. The second was to come up with a computer system to control and balance three different things – the motor, the battery and the engine.' There were many battery choices available, but there was no computer system that could be taken off the shelf and shoehorned into the Prius. The computer is the heart of the system's operation, determining the power flow and the recharging of the battery, and it would have to be developed in-house. Fortunately, Uchiyamada is also a software engineer.

There are twenty types of hybrid systems that could have been developed and used in the Prius, says Uchiyamada. 'We had these simulated on computers to figure out which one showed the best fuel efficiency. Then we narrowed it down to three systems. And we had to evaluate how appropriate they were for an actual product, its size, cost and productivity. That is how we picked the current hybrid system for the Prius.'

Once the decision was made on the type of hybrid system, Uchiyamada's team worked for two and a half years, he says, and 'at the height of the development stage team members were working seven days a week, twenty-four hours of a day in shifts'. The core full-time members of the Prius development team comprised of Uchiyamada and three others, plus about 1,000 engineers and others assigned in their departments to work on the Prius project. How does such a workforce not directly assigned to work for Uchiyamada work together as a team? Says

Uchiyamada, 'This is hard to explain to non-Toyota people, but it depends on how I can convince each engineer with my passion toward my work and on how much the real boss of that engineer is willing to share his manpower with me.' He had to admit his passion was persuasive enough to complete the job on time and on budget.

CHAPTER THIRTEEN
SUMMING UP: THE GO-IT-ALONE COMPANY

Toyota is a company that defies attempts to categorize it. For all its reverence for the founders and their ideals, and the constant repetition of their slogans, exhortations and admonitions, it is now a company striving to change, to adapt old precepts to a new world environment. It is becoming a true global company but is not there yet, even though it is multinational and manufactures on every continent. Although the outspoken and progressive Hiroshi Okuda says he can envision the day when board meetings will be held in the English language, the question of board membership for foreigners remains unanswered but seems unlikely in the foreseeable future. Foreign voices are heard every day in the handling of Toyota's affairs, and foreign ideas often prevail in doing Toyota's business abroad. Yet every top foreign executive abroad is doubled with a Japanese coordinator, a cumbersome and costly way to do business, which represents something less than a full show of confidence. For all that the Toyota executives who travel the globe on company business have worked and lived abroad, and can communicate freely with their counterparts in the industrial sphere, the inner working of the company is still largely opaque to outsiders, its decision-making process anything but transparent.

Yet Toyota is a well-run company, a paradigm in the world of industry. Its mission and corporate philosophy resonate with people in every corner of the earth and, as we have seen, foreigners who come to work for Toyota seem to find a humane logic in its operation.

Toyota is a financially powerful company and, in the face of the international move toward corporate alliances in the automobile industry, with its $25 billion economic cushion in the bank it is likely to be the suitor rather than the sought. Despite the siren song of next century technology, the company has not forgotten its core business. Prefabricated housing by Toyota is a nice sideline and new marine and aviation business ventures may add a bit of revenue. In its development of integrated transportation system concepts Toyota does not lose sight of the fact that it is automobiles that will remain its primary business. While major markets saturate with current model and increasingly obsolescent cars, replacement markets open up and new markets beckon. China and India, the two most populous nations on earth, are high on the company's agenda and, although the company has often been accused of moving slowly, Toyota, like the mills of the gods, grinds exceedingly fine.

When Toyota finally decided to make a luxury car it made a very good one that gave the smug Mercedes management a jolt. It is a car which continues to top the quality lists of the J. D. Power & Associates researchers survey after survey. Likewise, when a Detroit engineer set out to produce a new model car for Ford, he bought a Toyota Camry and set it before his team as his target for quality. A Chrysler minivan designer targeted the Toyota Previa. Toyota has of late begun, with projects like the Prius, to move ahead of the market curve, and with its ability to put a new car into production in a stunningly short eighteen months it has an enviable advantage.

But whether Toyota makes cars the market wants will continue to be the crucial point. It fights the image of being stodgy, of not having an immediately identifiable persona. As American industry critic Jerry Flint puts it, 'They still have a problem putting character into their cars, that intangible thing like the Mercedes star. If it's a Toyota it is going to be a good product, but not too exciting.' It is just this excitement that Toyota is trying to inject into its model line-up now, with cars like the Camry Solara, the new Celica, the Lexus SC300 and SC400, the Lexus LX470 SUV and the new Avensis.

Yet for all its success abroad, its fine-tuning of production and efforts to energize and upgrade its dealer network at home, Toyota is still tilting at the windmill of a 40 per cent share of the domestic market. The company reached its sales apogee of 43.2 per cent of the Japanese market in 1987 but has hovered tantalizingly just below 40 per cent since 1996, something Okuda vowed to correct shortly after he took over the previous year. The magic number remains elusive. Setting such a public goal could be a mistake, considering that almost certainly there will be more cars on the market from other makers, including foreign makes, in the months and years ahead. New Toyota models appealing to women and youth, sales events, free test-driving and more aggressive dealerships may be needed just to keep the company's current domestic market share. Still, a situation in which a low yen rate and firm overseas markets – North America and Europe – account for the year's profits, as in 1998, is not a healthy one. The results from the West were obviously doubly welcome after sales in Asia in 1998 plummeted by two-thirds in the wake of the currency crises in Indonesia, Thailand and elsewhere.

GETTING EVEN LEANER

Whether Toyota can make the moves that it seems dedicated to remains to be seen. Even though it is now the low-cost car producer, change is in the air, and even old timers like vice-chairman Iwao Isomura philosophize that 'Success is the mother of failure, and failure is the father of success.' He, for one, has been working on streamlining the company for ten years by abolishing what he called the 'log jam in middle management'. It was a project Okuda shoved into high gear. Now that the obstruction has been abolished it still remains to be seen whether younger managers given their head can bring the company back to its old leadership domestically against its many competitors.

'Toyota managers never give me the expected answers,' says University of Tokyo professor of economics Takahiro Fujimoto. 'Nissan managers are very friendly. If you use academic jargon they can talk about it. They read the books and know the things written about the industry and respect it because it is written by some famous American scholar. At Toyota the reaction is "So what!" They never give us the expected answers, they use their own vocabulary. They'll say, "Well, we don't know about 're-engineering' but we know what is good for the customers; if it is good for the customers we do it. We don't care who wrote the book."' This pugnacious attitude has brought the company a long way, and it reflects the way a pragmatic and flexible team of managers can look at new challenges with an open mind. Fiercely competitive, they tend to see everything they do in terms of improvement, of change, and ultimately of marketability. And they like to do it themselves.

Isomura began worrying about the levels of management a decade ago when he was in charge of personnel. 'Among the young people, being promoted to managerial level was considered success. I found that too many people were involved in making decisions, and it was very time-consuming. Revolutionary ideas were being rejected because of this log jam . . .' Under the old system, which still exists at many Japanese companies, decisions are made in a cumbersome manner which requires that consensus be gained from a large number of people. The flow of ideas from the top down and from the bottom up is often choked along the way by the need to get everybody's approval, and often decisions are made before the consensus is in.

'The problem with the old system,' continues Isomura, 'was that when you finally became a manager you wanted subordinates, and that made for inefficiency, but becoming a manager was the mark of success.' That needed changing. Isomura says there was considerable internal opposition to abolishing the middle management layer. The way it was finally accomplished was by establishing specialists in specific fields and giving them specialist training. 'They would receive their recognition inside and outside the company. They would have higher status, but without titles. After all, an engineer would rather be doing engineering work than be a manager but, before, they had to become a manager to be judged rightly. That was not their, nor our, intention.'

Contrary to the long-standing Japanese system in which individuals were moulded to company needs, in future, they believe at Toyota, that individuals and specialists, rather than generalists, will be sorely needed. The market moves so fast that there is no longer the luxury of years to train as there was in the past; results are needed quickly. Okuda, for one, is a believer that creativity is found more readily in the West than in Japan and that, to develop it in Japan, more emphasis must be placed on the individual.

Terukazu Inoue, Toyota's corporate auditor, joined the company out of law school but has never practised law for the company. Instead, like most of the older employees, he has held positions in several (four) different areas of the company. 'In our generation,' he says, 'the most versatile people were valued very highly in the company, people strong in ten different things, so to speak. But from now on we will need fast swimmers. Or even among the swimmers we will need short-distance swimmers, and long-distance swimmers, people with different strengths. We will be making efforts to come up with a match between certain jobs and individuals with an ability to perform that particular job best.' This is happening: the vertical structure of Japanese bureaucracies, universities and private companies is slowly being dismantled as the benefits of efficiency become obvious.

There is a risk, of course, as individualism hits Japan, and worker mobility increases while the population is ageing, that young workers will become scarce. Inoue believes that workers will stay with the best companies, but that it is important in the coming era for first-generation people not to stand in the way of the new people. 'Toyota people are always talking about this issue,' says Prof. Koichi Shimokawa of Hosei University.

Okuda wielded a broad-axe after he took over in 1995, took titles away from general managers at the age of fifty-five and from managers at fifty, and gave them new responsibilities. He retired older board members, and introduced incentives including stock options for executives. He revelled in being called 'The Destroyer'. And he also said he would not stay too long. In January 1999, the Japan Federation of Employers' Associations, known as Nikkeiren, announced that it would appoint Okuda its president at midyear. When Okuda takes the reins at Nikkeiren the way will open at Toyota for even more change. And if the recent past is the prologue, something practical will come from it, perhaps even a new and unorthodox alignment of top management and responsibilities.

'A youthful spirit and vitality' was an early Toyota slogan that Okuda likes to refer to as a guide for today. As for the future, he challenges his colleagues: 'If we dare to be as bold as the company founders we will get off to a flying start in the twenty-first century.'

Selected Bibliography

Collins, James C., and Porras, Jerry I., *Built to Last: Successful Habits of Visionary Companies*, HarperCollins, 1994.

Cusumano, Michael A., *The Japanese Automobile Industry: Technology & Management at Nissan & Toyota*, Council on East Asian Studies, Harvard University, Harvard University Press, Cambridge, MA, 1985.

Cusumano, Michael A., and Nobeoka, Kentaro, *Thinking Beyond Lean: How Project Management is Transforming Product Development at Toyota and Other Companies*, The Free Press, New York, 1998.

Fingleton, Eamonn, *Blindside: Why Japan is Still on Track to Overtake the U.S. by the Year 2000*, Houghton Mifflin Co., Boston and New York, 1995.

Fujimoto, Takahiro, 'An Evolutionary Process of Toyota's Final Assembly Operations', Discussion Paper Series, Faculty of Economics, University of Tokyo, Tokyo, 1996.

Kato, Seisi, *My Years with Toyota*, Toyota Motor Sales Co., Tokyo, 1981.

Keller, Maryann, *Collision: GM, Toyota, Volkswagen and the Race to Own the 21st Century*, Currency Doubleday, New York, 1993.

Mantle, Jonathan, *Car Wars: Fifty Years of Greed, Treachery, Skullduggery in the Global Marketplace*, Arcade Publishing, New York, 1995.

Miyashita, Kenichi, and Russell, David, *Keiretsu: Inside the Hidden Japanese Conglomerates*, McGraw Hill, New York, 1994.

Moritz, Michael, and Seaman, Barrett, *Going for Broke: The Chrysler Story*, Doubleday & Co., Inc., Garden City, NY, 1981.

Murphy, R. Taggart, *The Weight of the Yen: How Denial Imperils America's Future and Ruins an Alliance*, W.W. Norton, New York, 1996.

Ohno, Taiichi, *Toyota Production System: Beyond Large Scale Production*, Productivity Press, Portland, OR, 1988. (From Ohno, Taiichi, *Toyota seisan hoshiki*, Diamond Inc., Tokyo, 1978.)

Seidensticker, Edward, *Tokyo Rising: The City since the Great Earthquake*, Harvard University Press, Cambridge, MA, 1990.

Shimokawa, Koichi, Ed., *Toyota: History of the First 50 Years*, Toyota Motor Company, Tokyo, 1988.

Shnayerson, Michael, *The Car That Could: The Inside Story of GM's Revolutionary Electric Vehicle*, Random House, New York, 1996.

Thurow, Lester, *Head to Head: The Coming Economic Battle among Japan, Europe and America*, Warner Books, New York, 1993.

Togo, Yuki, *Sell Like Hell!!*, Toyota Motor Corporation, Tokyo, n.d.

Toyoda, Eiji, *Toyota: Fifty Years in Motion*, Kodansha International, Tokyo, New York, 1987. (From Toyoda, Eiji, *Watakushi no rirekisho*, Nihon Keizai Shimbunsha, Tokyo, 1985.)

Van Wolferen, Karel, *The Enigma of Japanese Power: People and Politics in a Stateless Nation*, Alfred A. Knopf, New York, 1989.

Walton, Mary, *Car: A Drama of the American Workplace*, W.W. Norton & Company, New York, London, 1997.

Womack, James P., Jones, Daniel T., and Roos, Daniel, *The Machine That Changed the World: The Story of Lean Production*, Rawson Associates, Macmillan Publishing Co., New York, 1990.

Womack, James P., and Jones, Daniel T., *Lean Thinking: Banish Waste and Create Wealth in Your Corporation*, Simon & Schuster, New York, 1996.

Yates, Brock, *The Critical Path: Inventing an Automobile and Reinventing a Corporation*, Little, Brown and Company, Boston, New York, 1996.

Chronology

1897	Sakichi Toyoda completes the Toyoda power loom
1918 Jan	Sakichi Toyoda establishes Toyoda Spinning & Weaving Co., Ltd.
1926 Nov	Toyoda Automatic Loom Works, Ltd. established
1933 Sept	Automobile Department established within Toyoda Automatic Loom Works
1934 Sept	First Type A Engine completed
1936 Apr	Production of the Model AA passenger car begins
Jul	Four G1 trucks exported to north-east China (first export shipment)
1937 Aug	Toyota Motor Co., Ltd. (TMC) established; Risaburo Toyoda appointed first president
1938 Nov	Koromo plant begins operation
1941 Jan	Kiichiro Toyoda appointed president
1946 Jan	Toyota Motor Koromo Labour Union formed
1947 Oct	Production of the Model SA passenger car begins
	Cumulative production vehicles 100,000 units
1950 Apr	Toyota Motor Sales Co., Ltd. (TMS) established; Shotaro Kamiya appointed president
Apr–Jun	First labour dispute
Jul	Taizo Ishida appointed president
1951 May	Creative Ideas and Suggestions System established
Aug	Model BJ 4WD vehicle marketed

1954 Jun	Model BJ 4WD vehicle named Land Cruiser
Oct	Toyota Technical Center building completed
1955 Jan	Crown marketed
1956 Apr	Multiple sales channel system begins; Toyopet dealer channel established
1957 Aug	Two sample Crowns exported to the US
Oct	Toyota Motor Sales, USA., Inc. established
1958 Jan	First overseas plant, Toyota do Brasil S.A., Industria e Comercio, begins operation
1959 Aug	Motomachi plant begins operation
Dec	Monthly production reaches 10,000 units
1960 Dec	Passenger car exports to the US temporarily halted
1961 Jun	Publica dealer channel (present Corolla dealer channel) established
Aug	Fukio Nakagawa appointed president
1962 Feb	TMS establishes Export Headquarters
Jun	Cumulative domestic production reaches 1,000,000 units
Sep	Toyota South Africa Motors (Pty.), Ltd. (TSAM) begins operation
1964 May	Nagoya Wharf Center completed
1965 Nov	TMC awarded the Deming Application Prize
1966 Sept	Takaoka plant begins operation
Oct	Business tie-up agreement signed between TMC, TMS, Hino Motors, Ltd. and Hino Motor Sales, Ltd.
Nov	Higashifuji Automobile Performance Testing Center (currently Higashifuji Technical Center) completed
1967 Oct	Toyota Auto dealer channel established Eiji Toyoda appointed president
Nov	Business tie-up agreement signed between TMC, TMS and Daihatsu Motor Co., Ltd.

1968 Oct	Monthly domestic production reaches 100,000 units
Dec	Annual domestic production reaches 1,000,000 units
1969 Apr	TMS Brussels Office opens in Belgium
Sept	Cumulative exports reach 1,000,000 units
1972 Jan	Cumulative domestic production reaches 10,000,000 units
Oct	Monthly domestic production reaches 200,000 units
Dec	Annual domestic production reaches 2,000,000 units
1973 Oct	Calty Design Research, Inc. established in the US
1974 Apr	Procurement of parts from overseas begins
Oct	Toyota Foundation established
1975 Dec	Seishi Kato appointed TMS president
1979 May	Cumulative exports reach 10,000,000 units
Jun	Sadazo Yamamoto appointed TMS president
1980 Jul	First service station completed in Beijing, People's Republic of China
Dec	Annual domestic production reaches 3,000,000 units
1981 Apr	Voluntary restraints exercised for car exports to the US
Jun	Shoichiro Toyoda appointed TMS president
1982 Jul	TMC and TMS merge to become Toyota Motor Corporation, with Eiji Toyoda, chairman; Shigenobu Yamamoto, vice-chairman; and Shoichiro Toyoda, president
1984 Feb	New United Motor Manufacturing, Inc. (NUMMI) established in joint venture with General Motors in the US
Oct	First phase of construction completed at the Shibetsu Proving Ground in Hokkaido

1986 Jan	Toyota Motor Manufacturing, USA., Inc. (TMM) established in the US (currently TMMK)
Jan	Toyota Motor Manufacturing Canada Inc. (TMMC) established in Canada
1987 Jun	Cooperative production agreement for the Hilux signed with Volkswagen AG of the Federal Republic of Germany
Aug	Establishment of new Lexus dealer network for luxury cars announced in the US
1988 May	First Camry off the line at TMM in the US
Dec	Annual domestic registration reaches 2,000,000 units
1989 Jun	N.V. Toyota Motor Marketing Services Europe S.A. (TMSE) established in Belgium (currently N.V. Toyota Motor Europe Marketing & Engineering S.A. (TMME))
Sept	Toyota Europe Office of Creation (Toyota EPOC) opens in Brussels
1992 Mar	DUO dealer channel opens (to handle VW and Audi vehicles)
Sept	Tatsuro Toyoda appointed TMC president
Dec	Toyota Motor Manufacturing (UK) Ltd. (TMUK) begins production
1993 Sept	Cumulative domestic production reaches 80,000,000 units
1995 Aug	Hiroshi Okuda appointed TMC president
1996 Oct	Toyota Motor Manufacturing North America, Inc. (TMMNA) established
1997 Jul	Virtual Venture Company (WC) established
1998 Jul	Production begins at Tianjin Toyota Motor Engine Co. Ltd. in China
Oct	Paris showroom, 'Le Rendez-Vous Toyota', opened

Dec   Toyoto Motor Manufacturing Indiana, Inc.
(TMMI) and Toyota Motor Manufacturing
West Virginia, Inc. (TMMWV) begin
production. Cumulative domestic production
reaches 97,200,000 units

Index